PROVERBS

A Bible Study
for Kids by Kids

THE NELSON KIDS

BTOZ PUBLISHING

Proverbs

By the Nelson Kids
(Blaise, Hope, and Silas Nelson)

Copyright 2011, by Blaise, Hope, and Silas Nelson
725 Montclair Dr.
El Paso, TX 79932
www.btozpublishing.com
www.premeditatedparenting.net

For the sake of clarification and consistency, we have chosen to capitalize personal pronouns that refer to God to avoid confusion, even when quoting from translations that do not follow this common practice.

Published by BtoZ Publishing

El Paso, Texas

ISBN # 978-1468005127

TABLE OF CONTENTS

Let's Get the Boring Stuff out of the Way

First of all, we would like to offer our thanks to you for choosing this book. Through it, we hope to bring your child or children closer to God. Our family has had family devotions for years. As some of the younger children started joining us in seeking the Lord, we came to realize that there aren't many good Bible studies for kids that take them all the way through a book of the Bible. There's stuff out there for adults, where you can go and pick up a study for the book of, say, 1 Peter. But there isn't much out there like that for kids. Though there are good devotions on *concepts* or *stories from the Bible,* there was nothing quite like this! Well, from that realization came the product that you are now holding. We wrote this book in order to help kids really understand a book of the Bible. We tried to make it as fun as possible for kids because we want them to have a love for the Bible, not a dread of it. With that being said, this is directed at young readers. There are activities, fun games, and questions. Our prayer is that this book would change lives and that after reading this book, your children would know, understand, and apply the stuff that they learn in Proverbs. We also hope that this is only the first book, and that more will follow. Here are a few questions that we would like to answer right off the bat:

"How do you deal with the adultery verses?"

Proverbs 5 - 7 contain a good deal of material dealing with the adulteress. It is referred to as "adult stuff" in the text. We don't go into detail but simply encourage the kids to be responsible with their lives. We mainly focus on verses that deal directly with children.

"How much work should my child do daily?"

Every child is very different. Some kids have no problem going through a chapter in 45 minutes, while others need a bit more time. With a few exceptions, each chapter is split up into three sections. Each section includes some text, several questions, and a fun game. There are two ways that we think would be reasonable to tackle this: #1 do a chapter a day or #2 do a section a day. Again, every situation is different. There is no set boundary on how to do this. Do what you feel would be best for your child and/or family.

"Is there an answer key to the questions from the text and the puzzles?"

Yes, there is an electronic version of the answer key available that contains all of the answers to the quizzes and games. The answer key is available at BtoZpublishing.com.

"Is the text translation dependent?"

No, the book is designed to be interchangeable between different translations of the Bible. The verses that are extensively talked about are included within the text. The translations used in this book are the NIV, NLT, NASB, KJV, and the NCV.

If you have any other questions, you can contact us at:

www.btozpublishing.com

Again, we hope that this book is a blessing to your family, and that your kids' lives will be changed. We pray that as the next generation is being raised up the torch would not be put out. The journey starts here. Now is their time. We pray that this will help give them the foundation that they will need throughout their lives.

PROLOGUE:

thE bEGiNNiNG thiNGY

Welcome to Proverbs! You're about to dive into one of the coolest books of the Bible. We're praying that this book will help you understand the book of Proverbs a little bit better. But even more so, we pray that this book will bring you a little closer to God. If it doesn't do that, then we have failed. So please, as you begin to go through this, come with listening ears. You just might hear God whisper something to you.

Before we begin, you'll notice that there are some crazy characters all over the place. We would like to get you familiar with them so that you know what they are there for. So with that meet:

Real Life

Pay attention whenever you see this dude around, because you're about to be given an action step.

BAD IDEA

Proverbs is a book of warnings against bad ideas. This little man is there to make sure that you see these warnings.

Who Knew?

The Bible is full of incredible facts and trivia. Watch for them when you see this guy around.

Study Up

This dude will show up whenever you're about to learn some practical ways to dig deeper into God's word.

Verse of Fame

Proverbs is full of "famous" verses. This guy will appear in every chapter to show you the famous verse.

Metal Man

This here is metal man. He's hiding once in every chapter. But be careful, because he might not always be doing the same thing, and he'll be harder to find as you go on.

With that, you're ready to go! Get ready to hear God speak to you and be ready to respond. Don't let this stuff go in one ear and out the other. This is the journey of a lifetime. So get ready to change your life!

CHAPTER 1:

YO! I'm Metal Man! Watch out for me! I'm hiding once in every chapter! I'll be doing different things.

The Beginning

And yes, you still have to find me again in this chapter!

Whoa! There's another me right up there

Go Read Proverbs 1:1-7

Ok, before we even begin this book, if you have already read these verses… good! You get an **A+** for listening and obeying. But if you skipped this section because you know it all, you're wise enough, blah, blah, blah; seriously, go read it! I promise you that you will get a lot more out of this book if you read the Bible along with it. So I'll give you a final chance on this ASSIGNMENT…

Go Read Proverbs 1:1-7 Again

Now that you have read these verses (hopefully), let's dig into the incredible book of Proverbs. There is a ton here to learn. Both Proverbs and Ecclesiastes were written by a dude named

Who Knew?

Proverbs is a book full of maxims. A maxim is a wise saying, like "An apple a day keeps the doctor away," or "Fish and visitors stink in three days," or "Read the chapter before you move on."

SOLOMON, **the son of the mighty King David. King** SOLOMON **was the wisest man who ever lived (except for Jesus… nice try). Let me tell you a little bit about** SOLOMON. **Some of** SOLOMON**'s greatest moments included asking God for wisdom instead of money, riches, or anything else (1 Kings 3); the judgment between the two mothers (1 Kings 3:16-28); and his building of the temple (1 Kings 5-6). Some** of his not-so-great moments occurred because of his 1,000 wives. Just so you know, there were a few other authors who contributed to Proverbs, but they don't write anything until the end of Proverbs, so we'll talk about them when we get there.

Quiz 1

1. Who is the first mentioned author of Proverbs? Who is his father?

2. What is a maxim? What is one maxim that you know?

3. What other book of the Bible was written by the guy who wrote the book of Proverbs? (You thought I was going to say his name, didn't you?)

4. What is one thing you learned from this section?

5. How are you going to apply what you learned today to your life?

Riddle Me This...

Puzzle #1 – *Poetic* PUZZLER

Read this poem out loud to a parent and circle the reference of the verse it is talking about.

This verse speaks about the wicked
And the color of BLOODY RED
And how they hurt only themselves
Take this lesson to your head

- Proverbs 1:1

- Proverbs 1:8

- Proverbs 1:18

- Proverbs 1:20

Verse of Fame

Proverbs 1:7

The fear of the LORD is the beginning of knowledge, but fools despise wisdom and instruction.

Go Read Proverbs 1:1-7 Again

One of the first things that you should notice about Proverbs is that there are a lot of hard-to-understand words. The introduction of Proverbs is one of the neatest parts of the book, because it tells us about all of the **cool** stuff that we can learn from Proverbs. What are some of the things that Proverbs will help you gain? Every once in a while you will see charts in this book (like the one below). Here is what you need to do: go look at the verse that I tell you to look at and complete the chart. Answer this question: "Proverbs can be used for...?" I'll do the first one for you. If you really need help, you can go ask your parents. They're pretty good at this stuff.

Verse:	Proverbs Can Be Used For:
1:2	gaining wisdom and instruction
1:2	
1:3	
1:3	
1:4	
1:4	
1:6	

There's a lot that Proverbs can help us with, isn't there?

Let's look closer at Proverbs 1:7:

> *The fear of the LORD is the beginning of knowledge, but fools despise wisdom and instruction. Proverbs 1:7 NIV*

Wow! What does it mean when it says that the fear of the Lord is the beginning of knowledge and wisdom? Well, the fear of the Lord is the understanding that God sees everything we do, and that there is always either a punishment or reward for every decision that we make. When we understand that God sees and actually responds to what we do, we will begin to live our lives very differently.

Anyway, this is our introduction to Proverbs. Keep this in mind: if you ever start to think, "Wow, Proverbs is really **boring**..." then go back and read the intro again so that you can remember what Proverbs is really for and what it can do for you.

Quiz 2

1. What does Proverbs mean when it talks about the "fear of the Lord" in verse 7?

2. What is one thing that you have used wisdom (Proverbs) for?

3. If you ever get bored of Proverbs, what should you do?

4. What is one thing you learned from this section?

5. How are you going to apply what you learned today to your life?

Riddle Me This...

<u>Puzzle #2</u> – Double Puzzle

Fill in the blanks with the word that belongs. Then put the circled letters in the blanks below.

_ _(_)_ _ O _   **- The author of most of**
1   **Proverbs**

D(_)_ _ _   **- The father of Proverbs'**
2   **author**

_ _(_)_ O _   **- Who cries out in the**
3   **streets? (Proverbs 1:20)**

_ _ U(_)_   **- Opposite of lies/what**
4   **wise people tell**

_ _ _ _ E _ _(_)   **- The book we are studying**
5

Wisdom __ __ __ __ __ forever
         1 2 3 4 5

14

Go Read Proverbs 1:8-19

Ok, let me GUESS what you think of when you read these verses. You see some big, hairy men that kind of look like giant, ugly trolls. Probably in your mind, you see these guys trying to get you to kill someone and take their money. Now, you might think that you will never, ever, in a gazillion years, see any of these guys— ever. And you probably won't. So, you're thinking that what you should really do is ignore this because it isn't aimed at you, but to people who live in

mountains (where trolls live). But wait a minute. This isn't what these verses are talking about; these verses actually hold something for all of us. What we need to get from this is the warning to watch out for people who try to lead us into making wrong choices. Now, it is true that these Proverbs are talking about people who try and get you to kill someone, but what it is really warning you about is people who try and get you to make *any* wrong decision, big or little. It could even be your friend who tells you to **swipe** a little bit of candy. We read at the end of this section where God

Real Life

Be careful to be like Jesus in everything you do. If someone tells you to do something that's not right, remember that God is watching and that He knows what you're doing.

sternly warns us that those who do wrong will be punished, *every single time*. You need to know that your friend will be punished for **swiping** candy one way or the other, and that you should never join a friend in doing things that are wrong. That's a *way* bad idea!

Go Read Proverbs 1:20-33

Why do you think that this picture of Wisdom, calling out into the street, appears right here in Proverbs? Well, we read that the man in the verses before this did not meet a very nice end to his life. Wisdom is saying the same thing; only this time, it happens to people who do not listen to Wisdom. We could guess that there might be a CONNECTION to not listening to wisdom and listening to fools. Those who do not listen to Wisdom will come to a bad end, while those who do listen to her are protected by her. When you live your life wisely, your choices will keep you from ruining your life. That's one way that wisdom will protect you. We are going to be seeing a lot of very similar things about this later in Proverbs. But, for right now, turn your ear to wisdom. Don't let your heart get distracted. And remember that God sees everything that you do. Every right choice that you make is seen by God, and it is going to be worth it to do the right thing every single time.

Quiz 3

1. According to Proverbs 1:18-19, what happens to evil men?

2. While foolishness destroys you, wisdom ___?___ you. (Proverbs 1:33)

3. Name one time when wisdom – knowing what is right – protected you.

4. What is one thing you learned from this section?

5. How are you going to apply what you learned today to your life?

SuperSpiesRUs.INC
321 SuperSneak Ln.
Hidden, Hiding 54321
1-800-ISPYONU

Top Secret
This Letter Permitted to
Authorized Personnel Only

Dear CodeCrusher:

Welcome to SuperSpies. I would tell you what we do, but that's a secret. We're pretty blunt in business here. So, here's what's up. Our enemies, WeGotTheSecret.INC (WidGeTS), love to receive information, commands, etc. about the Bible. So we need this information to help our SuperSpies train and grow in Jesus. However, they always code their messages so that no one can steal them. *You're* here to decode them for us. (You didn't see that coming, did you?)

We took this from WidGeTS headquarters. All we need to do now is decipher it. What we need you to do is "picture math." Like, if it's a picture of the sea, and then it says "- a + e", you should take off the "a" and add in the "e". So "Sea – a = Se" and "Se + e = See"

Good Luck,
Mr. SuperSneaky

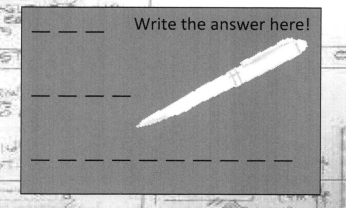

___ ___ ___   Write the answer here!

____ ____ ____ ____

____ ____ ____ ____ ____ ____

____ ____ ____ ____ ____ ____ ____ ____

 spelled backwards

's

Every + the – 🌸E + ○R – R

CHAPTER 2:

The Blessings of Wisdom

Go Read Proverbs 2:1-13

Do you remember how, in Chapter 1, God talked about some of the benefits of Wisdom? Well, in Chapter 2, Solomon and God talk more about these benefits.

Real Life

Next time you go on an Easter egg hunt, pray and ask God to give you a longing for wisdom.

Wow! It must be pretty important to Him for us to know the benefits of wisdom. Just how **hard** are we supposed to be looking for wisdom? Is this like a ho-hum type of looking? You know, the type of searching where you feel free to pick your nose while you're searching? (By the way, wisdom can help you with picking your nose too.) No! This type of searching comes with a desire. Do you remember at Easter time when you go hunt for those plastic eggs? You want to find as many as possible so that you can have as much candy as possible. When you see that pink egg hiding in the middle of the cactus plant, you just have to find some way to get it. Well, that's how you're supposed to look for wisdom. You're supposed to long for it, like you long to open presents on your birthday. Now, I know that this kind of longing is really, really hard to get, especially since wisdom isn't painted pink like those eggs. I know it's hard, but we really need to look for it so that we can make decisions in our lives that

18

honor God. One thing that you could do is pray that God gives you a desire to find wisdom and live in a way that pleases Him. You also have a map to help you find wisdom. It's called the Bible, and more specifically, the book of Proverbs! This is all working out pretty well, huh?

Quiz 4

1. How are we supposed to search for wisdom? (Proverbs 2:4)

2. Name one thing that you really long for.

3. What is our "map" that helps us find wisdom?

4. What is one thing you learned from this section?

5. How are you going to apply what you learned today to your life?

Riddle Me This...

<u>Puzzle #1</u> – WORD SEARCH

```
E   S   I   A   L   B   C   E   E   H   D
G   P   M   H   B   X   O   A   F   Y   J
A   P   B   W   U   Z   S   F   K   Q   C
H   C   I   T   K   T   L   M   S   X
G   S   B   R   E   V   O   R   P   A   X
E   W   L   R   Y   N   L   T   M   L   K
Q   G   E   B   G   D   O   J   A   I   X
J   G   M   I   X   A   M   R   V   S   G
G   H   N   M   K   V   O   X   O   K   V
E   G   D   M   C   I   N   D   I   F   M
E   P   O   H   C   D   K   N   G   K   A
```

Find these words in the puzzle:

Bible

David

Easter Egg

Longing

Maxim

Proverbs

Solomon

Wise

20

Go Read Proverbs 2:1-13 Again

Let's stick with Easter eggs. Why do you run around so fast when you look for those eggs? Is it because you really, really like Easter eggs, and like to sleep with Easter eggs, and when you grow up you want to be an Easter egg? Maybe, but probably not. What are you really looking for when you hunt for those Easter eggs? You're really looking for the candy inside those eggs, aren't you? It's not the eggs; it's what comes with the eggs. You can't get the candy without the egg. The same thing could be said for wisdom. Does God *really* want you to be as wise as possible? Or does He want you to live a life marked by good choices that come with wisdom? When you look for wisdom, what you are really looking for (but maybe you don't know it) are the blessings that come with wisdom. But you can't make those choices or get those blessings without wisdom. Where does wisdom come from? Check out verse 6:

Study Up!

Name some other things that you are motivated to do because of a certain reward.

_____

_____

Why do *you* think that God made us so that we love rewards? _____

_____

> For the Lord gives wisdom;
> from His mouth come knowledge and understanding.
> Proverbs 2:6 NIV

Wow! Wisdom comes from God! So when you look for wisdom; you are really looking for blessings, and those blessings come from God because wisdom comes from God. So when you look for wisdom, you're really looking for God. Wow. Let me clarify that: God does not equal wisdom. However, it is impossible to gain true wisdom without finding God; because only in God do we find true wisdom.

Quiz 5

1. Where does wisdom come from, according to Proverbs 2:6?

2. Is it possible to find wisdom without finding God?

3. Can you find God without finding true wisdom?

4. What is one thing you learned from this section?

5. How are you going to apply what you learned today to your life?

Riddle Me This...

Fill in the benefit mentioned in the verse we give you. So if the verse says, "If you obey wisdom you will have a small tax rate," you would write in the blank, "Small tax rate." And, no, that is not one of the answers.

Verse	Benefit
EXAMPLE	Small tax rate
2:5	
2:9	
2:12	
2:20	

Verse of Fame

Proverbs 2:7

He holds success in store for the upright, He is a shield to those whose walk is blameless.

23

Go Read Proverbs 2:1-13 (yes, *again*)

Now let's check out a couple of those blessings that Proverbs talks about. The two coolest blessings that pop up in this passage are the Lord's protection (verse 7) and a good direction for your life (verse 9).

> *He holds success in store for the upright,*
> *He is a shield to those whose walk is blameless...*
> *Proverbs 2:7 NIV*
> *Then you will understand what is right, just, and fair,*
> *and you will find the right way to go.*
> *Proverbs 2:9 NLT*

Those are some really cool verses. Let's take a closer look at them. The Lord's protection (shield) is a really powerful thing. Does this mean that you'll never ever get hurt? No, but it *does* mean that the Lord will protect your soul. He generally does this with His unending peace. The other major blessing is a good  path for your life. When you make right choices, good things will happen to you. Now God promises that these things will happen to you, but He doesn't say *when* they will happen. They could happen tomorrow or when you are super old or in heaven or anywhere in between. Just know that the good things He promises will happen.

You thought we would never get to the second part of this chapter, didn't you? Don't be ridiculous.

Go Read Proverbs 2:14-22

Ok, we've already read about the benefits of wisdom, and some of the bad things that come if you don't have wisdom. Well, God must be serious about the curses that come with rejecting wisdom, because they appear again here and will continue to appear in all of the rest of Proverbs. Look how Proverbs tells you to keep yourself away from the temptations that tell you to do what is wrong. If you seek wisdom, and make right choices, things will go well for you. You have to choose to run from those temptations. Hey wait a minute! We already saw that when we make right choices, we please God. Awesome! This is all tied to making choices that please God. Cool, huh? Let's review! We need to long for wisdom. Wisdom equals right choices. Right choices equal a protected life and a good direction for your life (blessings). Bad choices equal a train wreck for your future. Pretty simple, huh?

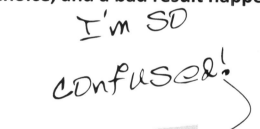

Quiz 6

1. When you make right choices, good things will happen to you. Name one time when you made a good choice, and there were good results.

2. Name one time when you made a bad choice, and a bad result happened.

I'm SO confused!

3. When does God fulfill his promises?

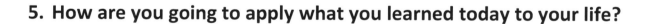

4. What is one thing you learned from this section?

5. How are you going to apply what you learned today to your life?

Decoding directions contained in the letter... (just read the letter below)

SuperSpiesRUs.INC
321 SuperSneak Ln.
Hidden, Hiding 54321
1-800-ISPYONU

Top Secret
This Letter Permitted to
Authorized Personnel Only

Dear CodeCrusher:

Alright, guess what. No, I didn't buy you the Decoder2000. No, I didn't buy you a strawberry banana smoothie. Alright, I'll just tell you. WidGeTS has been at their coding... *AGAIN.* We found this little scrap of paper in one of the spy's pillowcases. I can't make any sense of it. When we examined the spy's keyboard, the fingerprint on his space bar matches the fingerprint on the paper we found. It looks like he'd been pressing it a lot. My guess is that he added extra spaces in the clue and took out some. So I think that the best thing you could possibly do is put forward slashes in the clue (forward slash: "/"). Kind of like this...

I/a m/the/m ost/ awes om e/spy/e ver.

After you finish, go ahead and write out the answer on the white piece of paper.

Good Luck,
Mr. SuperSneaky

<u>**If you**</u>
_____
_____
_____
_____
_____
_____
_____
_____

Ifyo umakeg oodch oi cest heng oo dr esultsw illcome.B utifyo umake badde cis ionsth enba d th ingsw ill co me. Wha ty oudoaff ects you rc onse quen ses.

CHAPTER 3: ADVICE FOR...

Go Read Proverbs 3:1-13

Who Knew?

Proverbs was written to kids, but did you know that only one book in the Bible was written to a woman? Can you guess which one it is? It's not Esther or Ruth... believe it or not, it's actually 2 John. Huh, who knew?

Ok, guys, this is where **PROVERBS** starts becoming super useful to us. Proverbs 1 told us that those who have done evil always come to destruction

and those who **HAVE** rejected Wisdom's call come to a bad end. Proverbs 2 told us that when we search for wisdom, we are actually searching for God and for the blessings that come from having wisdom. **FINALLY**, we come to the stuff that we can apply more easily in our lives. Believe it or not (you should consider believing it), Proverbs was actually written to... kids! But, you'll have to wait until Chapter 4 to find out

MORE about that. Because Proverbs was written to kids, you can already start to practice the things that we learn **ABOUT** in Proverbs.

COOL, huh? You don't have to wait until you're really, really old to start applying Proverbs; you can start right now!

Ok, I want you to pay close attention to verses 3, 5, 6, 7, 9, and 11. These are the things that you really need to remember. In these verses, Proverbs starts to teach you how TO be wise. Check out how most of these verses deal directly with your relationship with God. In order to fully understand wisdom, you need to have a strong and healthy relationship with God. If you listen to these Proverbs, they can really teach you how to keep up a healthy and strong relationship with God.

Now, what is Proverbs 3:11-12 SAYing?

> *My son, do not despise the LORD's discipline, and do not resent His rebuke, because the LORD's disciplines those He loves, as a father the son he delights in. Proverbs 3:11-12 NIV*

Do you ever get into trouble with your parents and they discipline you? Let me ask you a question: why do your parents discipline you? Is it because they are being mean and cruel, or because they love you? I know what you're thinking but let me tell you that your parents discipline you because they love you. When they DISCIPLINE you, it is because *you* (not them) made a poor choice and they are trying to help you not do it again. They're doing this because they know that bad choices WILL harm you. Trust me; they generally know what is best. Why do you think God disciplines us? Could it be for the same reason? According to this verse, God punishes people that He really loves, because He knows that when He punishes them, He is helping them become better people. Cool, huh? Now let me just tell you this. God does not hesitate to discipline us, yet not every bad thing that He allows to happen to us is a punishment. Sometimes He lets trouble happen to us so that we will draw closer to Him. Just know that everything that happens to you, as long as you are a Christian, will eventually lead to good; whether it is a punishment or just some hard times (Romans 8:28).

28

Quiz 7

1. What do you need in order to fully understand wisdom?

2. When a dog bites someone, the owner usually punishes it, so that it doesn't bite again. How is this like our parents disciplining us? (And, no, I'm not calling you a dog.)

3. Name one instance (situation) in which you did something, but after you were disciplined for it, you didn't do it again.

4. What is one thing you learned from this section?

5. How are you going to apply what you learned today to your life?

Riddle Me This...

Puzzle #1 – THE BOARD GAME

Did you notice all of those strange words and parts of words that looked like they were written on BOARDS? Find all of the BOARD words in this sections reading and put them in the blanks. As you read through the text, the first BOARD word you find should be written in the blank over the number 1. Put the next BOARD word you find over the number 2. Good luck!

_____ _____ _____ _____ _____ _____
   1   8   2   3   5   6

_____ _____ .
   4   7

Verse of Fame

Proverbs 3:5-6

Trust in the LORD with all your heart and lean not on your own understanding; in all your ways submit to Him, and He will make your paths straight.

30

Go Read Proverbs 3:14-20

This sounds kind of familiar, doesn't it? Wisdom comes with a lot of blessings. Let's take a quick look at some of the blessings that are shown here. Have you ever dreamed about finding a treasure chest or maybe a cave that is full of GOLD and silver? (Without pirates of course, let's not be having nightmares.) That sounds cool doesn't it? Imagine having something like 303 gazillion dollars. That's a lot of Happy Meals®! Anyway, do you remember why wisdom is as cool  as (or even cooler than) 303 gazillion dollars, silver, or GOLD? Take some time... go back and read Chapter 2 if you have to... OK, why is wisdom cool? Wisdom is so valuable because, when we search out wisdom, which comes from God, we are seeking God. Remember this? It's not the wisdom; it's that God is behind the wisdom. Check out these next two verses really quickly:

> *By wisdom the LORD laid the earth's foundations,*
> *by understanding He set the heavens in place;*
> *by His knowledge the deeps were divided,*
> *and the clouds let drop the dew. Proverbs 3:19-20 NIV*

Wow! Do you know what tools God used to make the whole world? Wisdom and power. How **cool** is that?

Quiz 8

1. Name three things that you really like. Is wisdom better than these things?

2. Why is wisdom so important?

   What does infinite mean? Flip to Chapter 8 (page 72) and look at the "Who Knew" to find out!

3. What is one thing that verses 19-20 tell us that God used his infinite wisdom for?

4. What is one thing you learned from this section?

5. How are you going to apply what you learned today to your life?

Riddle Me This...

<u>Puzzle #2</u>– THE GRAY GAME

All of these words have been scrambled. You have to unscramble them, and then write out the correct word underneath it. To give you a hint, the first letter of every word a lighter gray.

ETH LGNSSBSIE FO DMWSOI REA KILE RTEEASUR.

____ _____ __ _____ ___ ____ _____.

HYTE HACNEG URYO FILE.

_____ _____ ____ ____.

Go Read Proverbs 3:21-35

Check out all of those action steps from today's reading! Read these verses with me. Ready, go!

> *My son, do not let wisdom and understanding out of your sight, preserve sound judgment and discretion. Proverbs 3:21 NIV*

This verse tells us more blessings that come from wisdom, but it gives us two things that we are supposed to do in order to keep them. What are they? Read the verse again to find your answers!

1) <u>Do not let</u> _____

2) <u>Preserve</u> _____

 I won't answer that question because you just might see that in one of the questions at the end. Anyway, remember to keep those two things solid in your mind.

Check out verses 27-30. Proverbs is teaching us how we should treat others. Do you remember the GOLEN RULE that Jesus gave to us in Matthew 7:12?

> *So in everything, do to others what you would have them do to you, for this sums up the Law and the Prophets. Matthew 7:12 NIV*

Well, these verses are kind of like that. If you follow the Golden Rule, then you shouldn't have to worry too much about plotting against your neighbor, because if you follow the GOLEN RULE, you are obeying these verses.

Verses 31-35 introduce a method of writing that is used throughout the rest of Proverbs. Now don't fall out of your seat, but that method is called comparison. Comparison means taking two completely different things and looking at the *differences* that make them different. For example, most of Proverbs compares the righteous man and the wicked man. It also compares the wise man and the foolish man. What is compared in this section? (That also might be a question that you'll find at the end of this section...)

One last thing that I want to take a look at is verse 31.

> Do not envy a man of violence
> and do not choose any of his ways. Proverbs 3:31 NASB

Real Life

Why is this verse in the Bible? And what does envy mean? Well, this verse is saying not to be *jealous* of the wicked. Sometimes it is really easy to look at a wicked person and wish that you could do what they are doing, watch what they are watching, listen to what they are listening to, or say what they are saying. Well, this verse tells us that those people will not end up in a good spot if they continue down the road

What the wicked do is not always fun. If you look closely at the result of their actions, they are not good. Choose to do what is right.

that they're on. Just remember this verse the next time you feel like you're missing out on what the wicked are doing. Things will go *way* better for you if you follow God.

Quiz 9

1. What two things are compared in this section? (Proverbs 3:33-35)

2. What are the two things in verse 21 we have to remember in order to keep the blessings of wisdom?

3. What do Proverbs 3:27-28 and Matthew 7:12 have in common?

4. What is one thing you learned from this section?

5. How are you going to apply what you learned today to your life?

You'll continue to learn about the wicked man throughout the rest of Proverbs.

Puzzle #3– Code Crusher

Decoding directions contained in the letter... (just read the letter below)

Across

2. The book we are studying

3. Something that happens after we have been bad

5. Something Proverbs talks about a lot

6. Something that God wants us to have with him

Down

1. Something that we shouldn't hate

4. The reason God disciplines us

SuperSpiesRUs.INC
321 SuperSneak Ln.
Hidden, Hiding 54321
1-800-ISPYONU

Top Secret
This Letter Permitted to
Authorized Personnel Only

CONFIDENTIAL

Dear CodeCrusher:

We snagged this little goodie right out from under their noses. I hope this information is useful to us. Now, I have reports that this puzzle represents how everything in Proverbs "fits together". So what I think you should do is write the words into the puzzle according to the clues on the other paper. I guess whoever wrote this got bored. Man, what a terrible artist!

Good Luck,
Mr. SuperSneaky

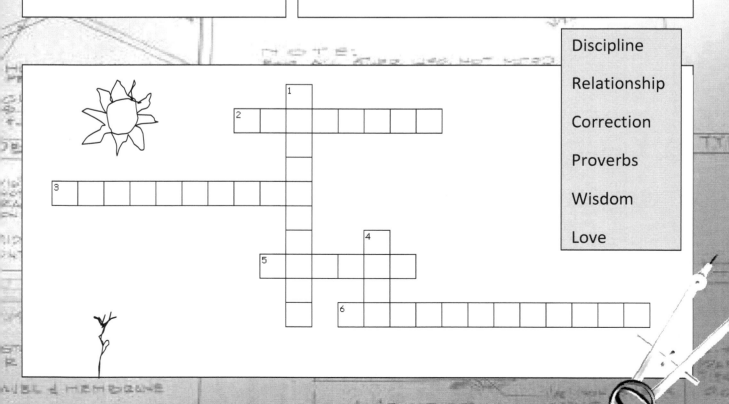

Discipline

Relationship

Correction

Proverbs

Wisdom

Love

CHAPTER 4:

LISTEN UP, KIDDO...

Go Read Proverbs 4:1-9

Are you still reading the Bible along with this book? It is really important to make sure that you know what I am talking about! OK, do you remember how I said that Proverbs was *written* for kids? Check out how much Solomon says "my son". He says it several times in this chapter, a lot in the first three chapters, and a lot more in future chapters. It's fair to guess that most of Proverbs was *written* either to Solomon's actual sons, or it was *written* to young people in general. Either way, since Solomon says "my son" all of the time, we can assume that it was *written* to people a lot younger than Solomon. This means that you'd better listen up! In these groups of verses, Solomon is talking to his actual children. When reading Proverbs, it is important to picture what is going on. Here's what I picture: I see a wise old king (I don't know whether or not Solomon was old when he wrote Proverbs; I just picture him that way). He's got this big white beard, he's sitting in a rocking chair, (I know the rocking chair wasn't invented yet. Use your imagination!) and his

Who Knew?

Did you know that Solomon's son's son's son's son's... well, for time's sake, just add a couple more "son's" and you'll get to a guy named Joseph. And guess who Joseph's son was? Jesus! Pretty cool, huh?

children are circled all around him. As he waves his wrinkled FINGER, he says, "Getting wisdom is the wisest thing you can do!" (NLT) OK, let me ask you an important question: who do you think is wiser - your grandpa, or the neighbor boy? Obviously, your grandpa is wiser, right? Why? Because your grandpa is older than the neighbor boy. So? Well, (in most cases) with age comes wisdom. When you're old, you've seen a lot of things in life. Now, we've already talked about the results of bad choices played out in people's lives, and you've seen the results of good choices. For example, you've lived long enough to know that spaghetti is way, way better tasting than spinach. Older people have lived long enough to see much more important stuff. Why is this important (about the old man, not the spaghetti)? This is a key thing to know because the guy talking in the beginning of Proverbs 4 is old. It's actually Solomon's father (King David) who's talking. When David says that wisdom is a far better choice than foolishness, he knows what he is talking about because he has seen the results of both good and bad choices in people's lives. David was called a "man after God's own heart." So he got to see firsthand the effects of good decisions in his life. But he also made some really bad choices, which led to the eventual death of three of his kids. Listen to these Proverbs, because David knew what he was saying!

Quiz 10

1. Who was Proverbs *written* to?

2. What is the first thing that Solomon's dad tells him? (Hint: Proverbs 4:4)

3. Just because someone's old, does that mean that they're really wise? Explain.

4. What is one thing you learned from this section?

5. How are you going to apply what you learned today to your life?

Verse of Fame

Proverbs 4:13

Hold on to instruction, do not let it go; guard it well, for it is your life.

Riddle Me This...

Puzzle #1 – NUMBER CODE

Break the code by filling in the blanks.

A	15
D	1
E	6
F	14
G	9
H	7
I	8
L	3
O	22
P	13
R	16
S	18
T	10
U	25

___ ___ ___   ___ ___ ___ ___

10   7   6   13   15   10   7

___ ___   ___ ___ ___

22   14   10   7   6

___ ___ ___ ___ ___ ___ ___ ___ ___

16   8   9   7   10   6   22   25   18

___ ___ ___ ___ ___

3   6   15   1   18

___ ___   ___ ___ ___ ___

10   22   3   8   14   6

40

Go Read Proverbs 4:10-19

In these next ten verses of Proverbs 4, the father (the old man) is talking to his children. Proverbs 4:18-19 contains another comparison, this one comparing the path of the wicked and the path of the righteous.

> *The path of the righteous is like the morning sun,*
> *shining ever brighter till the full light of day.*
> *But the way of the wicked is like deep darkness;*
> *they do not know what makes them stumble.*
> *Proverbs 4:18-19 NIV*

Remember how we talked about how older people have had the chance to see people's choices play out in their lives? Well, this is exactly what is being described in these verses. *Write* down the things that mark the path of the

wicked and the things that mark the path of the righteous based on those verses: (Look at the verses above for your answers!)

Path of the Righteous

Proverbs 4:18 - _

Path of the Wicked

Proverbs 4:19 - _

Pretty big difference, huh? Which path would you rather be on? The best part is that you get to choose. It's up to you.

Quiz 11

1. What two things does this section compare?

2. Describe the path of the righteous.

3. Describe the path of the wicked.

4. What is one thing you learned from this section?

5. How are you going to apply what you learned today to your life?

ARE YOU STILL REMEMBERING TO FIND METAL MAN? HE'S HIDING ONCE IN EVERY CHAPTER.

Riddle Me This...

<u>Puzzle #2</u> – **matchmaker**

Each of the words on the right can be matched to either the path of the righteous or the path of the wicked. Draw a line from the descriptive words to the path.

- Bright
- Slippery
- Right
- **Dark**
- Watched by God
- Wrong
- Death
- Life
- **No Peace**
- **Aimless**
- Has purpose
- Just
- **Peaceful**
- **Unjust**

Path of the Righteous •

Path of the Wicked •

43

Go Read Proverbs 4:20-27

Ok, let's take a look at verses 23-27, because they seem to be written especially for you:

> *Above all else, guard your heart, for everything you do flows from it. Keep your mouth free of perversity; keep corrupt talk far from your lips. Let your eyes look straight ahead; fix your gaze directly before you. Give careful thought to the paths for your feet and be steadfast in all your ways. Do not turn to the right or the left; keep your foot from evil.*
> *Proverbs 4:23-27 NIV*

Those verses tell you to watch your heart, mouth, eyes, and feet. What's this all mean? Are you supposed to be constantly making sure your heart's still pumping, you can still sing, your eyes can still see, and your feet still move? Probably not. That's not a very wise explanation, is it? It means to keep yourself from evil, period. This is telling you that your heart needs to focus on worthy things; your speech needs to be what is true; your eyes need to keep from looking at evil; and your feet need to stay away from places that you know will lead you to harm. Remember: making right choices is the result of having wisdom. Making right choices, following God, staying away from evil: it's all part of being wise.

Real Life

If you catch yourself doing something wrong today, tell a parent and then go do something kind and caring for someone else.

Quiz 12

1. What does Proverbs 4:23 tell us to do and why?

2. Name one time when you stayed away from evil.

3. What are a few things that we can do to stay away from evil?

4. What is one thing you learned from this section?

5. How are you going to apply what you learned today to your life?

Puzzle #3 – *Code Crusher*

Decoding directions contained in the letter... (just read the letter below)

SuperSpiesRUs.INC
321 SuperSneak Ln.
Hidden, Hiding 54321
1-800-ISPYONU

CONFIDENTIAL

Top Secret
This Letter Permitted to
Authorized Personnel Only

Dear CodeCrusher:

Here's our latest catch. We found this slipped under CodeMaker's dresser. He must have been trying to hide it. On the piece of paper, he wrote that they get useful information by applying the answer to this puzzle to their lives. The paper below has a bunch of pictures and words. I think that you've already done this before, but if you need help, take a look at the very first letter I sent you.

Good Luck,
    Mr. SuperSneaky

We use this little secret to get useful information.

CHAPTER 5: Going in Circles?

Go Read Proverbs 5

OK. Catch your breath. It *is* true that Proverbs is written for kids, but some parts of Proverbs are written for older kids or even adults! When these sections pop up, we just need to figure out what we can apply to *our* lives (at least until we are a bit older). Let's look at what we can apply from this section. The beginning of this chapter tells adults to be responsible with their lives. Even at our age, we can apply this by remembering that we need to be responsible with our lives and the choices that we make. The other areas that are most appropriate for us in this chapter are in verses 21-23:

Go Back and Reread Proverbs 5:21-23

These verses are really important for us to understand. Do you remember what the fear of the Lord is? It happens when we understand that God sees everything that we do. That's one part of it, but also remember that He has a response to what we do. Think I'm CRAZY? Well, let's reread verses 21-23 one last time:

> For your ways are in full view of the LORD,
> and He examines all your paths.
> The evil deeds of the wicked ensnare them;
> the cords of their sins hold them fast.
> For lack of discipline they will die,
> led astray by their own great folly.
> Proverbs 5:21-23 NIV

It not only says that God sees what we do but that He examines (or studies) our actions too. That's pretty powerful. Why does Solomon tell us this? I mean, we all know that God sees everything that we do, but why do we need to know that He *studies* our actions? Solomon is warning us to be careful in what we do because God responds to our actions. That's why he tells us this. Remember this: Proverbs is really a book that is looking at the penalties or rewards of our choices.

Who Knew?

"Consequence" is a fancy word for result. Like if you throw a cell phone on the ground, the consequence is a broken cell phone. If you are "responsible" for a consequence, you made it happen, and you own it.

Quiz 13

1. Define the word "responsibility".

2. Define the word "consequence".

3. What is one thing that verses 1-20 can teach us until we are older? (Reread the very first section in this chapter if you have to.)

4. What is one thing you learned from this section?

5. How are you going to apply what you learned today to your life?

Riddle Me This...

Puzzle #1 – THAT CONSEQUENCE GAME

Draw a line to connect the matching actions and consequences.

Licking an outlet •

Breaking a window •

Obeying God •

Smiling at others •

Hitting your friend in
the head with a
baseball bat

Being lazy •

Not feeding your dog •

• Rewards in Heaven

• A very unhappy puppy

• Discipline from your
parents

• A lot of work to do later

• A smile back

• A fried tongue

• A bunch of glass to clean
up *and* finding someway to
get the money to pay for it

Go Read Proverbs 5:21-23 Again

These verses are telling us that God sees everything we do. Remember that Solomon is telling us this so that we would remember that God has a response to our actions. Also remember that the fear of the Lord is remembering that God sees everything we do and that He will either punish us or reward us for it. Ok, real quick, let's look at another definition of THE FEAR OF THE LORD. (Because I am going to give you another definition, the old one will look like THIS, and the new one like THIS.) When we understand that GOD SEES OUR ACTIONS AND THAT HE HAS A RESPONSE TO THEM, we are recognizing that GOD GIVES US CONSEQUENCES FOR EVERY ACTION THAT WE DO, whether they are good or bad. Now what is the BEGINNING OF WISDOM, according to Proverbs 1:7? _ .

So, now we know that the BEGINNING OF WISDOM is understanding that GOD GIVES US CONSEQUENCES FOR OUR ACTIONS because understanding that GOD GIVES US CONSEQUENCES is the same as THE FEAR OF THE LORD.

Remember that since the BEGINNING OF WISDOM is FEAR OF THE LORD, we need to be responsible with our lives so that God will give us good consequences at the end of our lives. Since we are looking for good consequences, we want to make wise and responsible choices, which is the same as being wise. Confused? So am I. I hope that this picture will help you understand this...

This chart shows how all of these things impact the each other. The arrows mean that one thing leads to the next.

Fear of the Lord

Beginning of Wisdom

Understanding that there are consequences for our actions

Even though they are all different, these things are all the same thing.

50

Quiz 14

1. What is the first definition we gave you of the FEAR OF THE LORD?

2. What is the second definition of the FEAR OF THE LORD?

3. What is the beginning of wisdom according to Proverbs 1:7?

4. What is one thing you learned from this section?

5. How are you going to apply what you learned today to your life?

Verse of Fame

Proverbs 5:21

For your ways are in full view of the LORD, and He examines all your paths.

Real Life

Have one time today when you take responsibility for an action and its consequence. Like, if you draw on the wall, say, "I drew on the wall and will take the consequence of cleaning all the marks off."

Puzzle #2 – *Code Crusher*

Decoding directions contained in the letter... (just read the letter below)

Lord

1. _ _ _ _
2. _ _ _ _
3. _ _ _ _
4. _ _ _ _

SuperSpiesRUs.INC
321 SuperSneak Ln.
Hidden, Hiding 54321
1-800-ISPYONU

Top Secret
This Letter Permitted to
Authorized Personnel Only

CONFIDENTIAL

Dear CodeCrusher:

Someday, we'll have *you* break into WeGotTheSecret's headquarters; there were five guards we had to get past! Anyway, all that matters is that we got these things out of that envelope below. So, what I think you should do is follow the directions on the piece of white paper below. In the end, you should come up with a word that is closely related to the original word.

Good Luck,
Mr. SuperSneaky

FOR LORD:

IN FIRST BLANK, WRITE OUT THE WORD LORD, BUT CHANGE OUT THE "D" WITH AN "R". YOUR FIRST BLANK SHOULD SAY, "LORR". IN THE SECOND BLANK, WRITE LORR, BUT CHANGE THE "O" TO AN "E". IN THE NEXT BLANK, WRITE THE SAME THING YOU JUST WROTE, EXCEPT, CHANGE THE FIRST "R" TO "A". LASTLY, WRITE THE SAME THING THAT YOU JUST WROTE, BUT CHANGE THE "L" TO AN "F".

CHAPTER 6:

SLUGGARDS, DEBTORS, & ANTS, Oh My!

Go Read Proverbs 6:1-5

The end of Proverbs 6 and all of Proverbs 7 are written for adults, but we will try to get as much from them as we can. Proverbs 6 begins with a warning. This

Real Life

To avoid getting into debt, wait to buy something you want until you actually have money for it. That way, you won't need to borrow money from others.

might seem like a weird commandment at first, but hopefully it will make sense very soon. First of all, what is Solomon warning us about? He warns us against taking up security for a debt.

Ok, what does it mean to take up security for a debt? Well, imagine that you have a friend who wants to buy a really nice car, so he goes to the bank and asks if he can borrow money. (YES, you can borrow money from the bank, and NO, you may not!) Well, the bankers laugh and scoff at him, saying, "Ha! Yeah right! You're just a kid! What's a ten year old need a car for anyway?" So he comes to you and he's like, "Dude, I can't buy my

car." So you go to the bank and say, "Look, my friend Billy Bobby Jones here is a great guy. In fact, he's so great that if you give him money, and he can't pay it back, I'll pay it for him." Well, guess what? Billy Bobby Jones doesn't pay back the money and you're stuck paying $50,000 for a car that's not even yours. Sounds like fun, doesn't it? Go get your piggy bank; you're gonna need it!

Ok, do you see what taking up security for a debt is? It is when you say that if someone can't pay back something, you'll pay it back for them. Now, why does the book of Proverbs say that this is a bad idea? Well, because it can go really bad for you. It might seem like a good idea at first, but if you're wrong, then you're sunk.

Now there is a big difference between being generous and what Proverbs is talking about here. Being generous means helping someone in need. Taking security for a debt is putting yourself in danger for something that is not worth putting yourself in danger for. Now, I know that, in no way whatsoever, you are even thinking about buying a car, taking up security for a debt, or cheese (I bet you're thinking about cheese now). This seems to be more for adults, but just remember it for when you get older. If you ever find yourself in that situation, GET OUT as fast as you can, before something bad happens. Proverbs clearly tells us that this is not a risk worth taking. Sure, this situation might not end badly, but why take that risk?

Quiz 15

1. Explain the act of taking up security for a debt.

2. Why is it a bad idea to take up security for a debt?

3. What should you do if you find yourself in a "security for a debt" situation?

4. What is one thing you learned from this section?

5. How are you going to apply what you learned today to your life?

Riddle Me This...

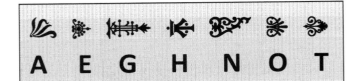

A	E	G	H	N	O	T

Puzzle #1 – Three Step Chaos

Okay, this is going to get complex, but we'll do this in three steps. Here's step one.

STEP #1 – First of all, take the information above and solve the puzzle to the right. This verse will give you a sneak peak into the next section!

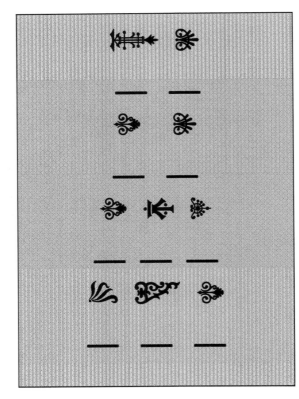

STEP #2 – Now, if you haven't noticed this already, the phrase that you revealed in step one is actually part of a verse in Proverbs 6. Find out which verse it is and write it in the blank.

Proverbs 6:__

This is your secret number!

STEP #3 – Alright. Now take your secret number that you wrote in the blank. Start at page 53 (the one that says Sluggards, Debtors, Ants, Oh My!) and count the title page as one, and then the next side of a page as 2, the next side as 3, and so on until you reach your secret number. You'll find that someone at the bottom of the page is saying something very odd. Since he's asleep, he's mumbling. Cross out all of the *m*'s, and you'll have your secret phrase.

_ _ _ ' _ _   _ _ _ - _ _ _ _ _   _ _   _ _ _

_ _ _   _ _ _ _ _ _ _   _ _ _ _ _ _

Go Read Proverbs 6:6-19

What does it mean to be **LAZY**? It means being a slacker, a lazybones, and generally not moving very much. Is this the only definition? OK, let me ask you a question: if your mom asks you to do something, do you ever put it off? Do you ever tell your mother something like, "Just a minute"? OK, is this the same as being **LAZY**? Do you know what *procrastination* (pro-crass-tin-nation) means? It is the process of putting a task off until later, kind of like... never mind. I'll explain it tomorrow. Well, you can think of procrastination as the same as laziness (maybe a little less than laziness, but it is still being lazy). So do you ever practice procrastination? Do you ever wait on doing your chores, and they never seem to get done? What do these

Who Knew?

Procrastination means to put off something until a time when you want to do it (which usually ends up being about 18 seconds before it needs to be done). Procrastination is a bad idea.

verses say about someone who is **LAZY**? There is a funny word in this passage. See if you can find it. It's not slumber... or overseer... Did you find it? Sluggard! What a weird word! It is basically the same as a lazybones. What does Proverbs tell the sluggard to do? It tells him to go look at an ant! Why? Well, have you ever watched those little guys carry a large piece of food? Have you seen them looking for a piece of food? Have you ever seen them attack an animal or your feet when their homes are ruined? Have you ever seen them sleeping and doing nothing? If you said yes to that last one, let me share a secret with you: you just stomped on him. That's why he's not doing anything. But think about it! Those little guys are always moving; they are never **LAZY** unless they're dead. God wants us to be hard-working, not lazy slackers or procrastinators. If we are hard workers, things will go well for us. Be a hard worker, like the ant.

The rest of this section deals with wicked people. Real quickly, let me explain the stuff that the Lord hates. The Lord clearly hates the actions of the wicked. Keep in mind that the Lord doesn't hate the *people*; He hates their *actions*. God hates all of our sins. When we sin, we hurt our relationship with God. But God still loves us. We'll take a look at that a bit later.

Quiz 16

1. What is procrastination?

2. What does Ephesians 6:7 tell us about work?

3. Is it ever OK to serve halfheartedly? Why or why not?

4. What is one thing you learned from this section?

5. How are you going to apply what you learned today to your life?

Ymomu're monme-fifmth omf tmhe wamy thmroumgh mPrmoverbs!

Riddle Me This...

Puzzle #2 – Double Puzzle

Put in the correct words where they belong. Put the circled letters in the order they come in the blanks at the bottom of the page in order to finish a sentence.

People who are in debt- ___ ___ ___ (O) ___ ___ ___

Something you can drive (and get in debt for) -

___ ___ (O) ___

What you buy ice cream with- ___ (O) ___ ___ ___

Someone who doesn't work very much-

___ ___ (O) ___ ___ ___ ___ ___

The book we are studying- ___ ___ ___ ___ ___ (O) ___

The main author of the book we are studying-

___ ___ (O) ___ ___ ___ ___

Something that mice really like- ___ ___ ___ ___ (O)

What does taking up security for a debt cause?

___ ___ ___ ___ ___ ___

Cars
Cheese
Debtors
Money
Proverbs
Solomon
Sluggard

Go Read Proverbs 6:20-35

How am I supposed to fit this entire scroll into the box on my forehead?

This is another one of those adult moments. However, let's not miss the first couple verses of this part of the chapter. These verses are telling you to listen to your parents. Listen to what your parents say, because remember, they are a lot wiser than you are.

What does it mean to bind something? It means to tie it up. So what does it mean to bind commands, laws, and teachings to yourself? Some people **THINK** that it literally means tying little boxes to your forehead with the commands written in them. (Have you ever noticed the Pharisees in the movies about Jesus? Those little boxes on their foreheads actually had commandments in them. You thought it was a *fashion* thing, right?)

God doesn't really want you to tie little boxes to your head. What He really wants is for you to always remember His commands whenever you make a decision. Now, you could tie little boxes to your forehead if you really wanted to; but, all you need to do is to never forget these commands (memorizing his commands helps a lot with that). Trust me; they will come to mind when you need them the most.

Quiz 17

1. What does it mean when it talks about binding commandments onto yourself?

2. Name one time when you memorized a verse.

3. Name one time when a verse that you had memorized helped you in a situation.

4. What is one thing you learned from this section?

5. How are you going to apply what you learned today to your life?

Verse of Fame

Proverbs 6:6

Go to the ant, you sluggard; consider its ways and be wise!

Decoding directions contained in the letter… (just read the letter below)

ANSWER:

Proverbs 6:6

Proverbs 6:19

Proverbs 6:20

Proverbs 6:21

SuperSpiesRUs.INC
321 SuperSneak Ln.
Hidden, Hiding 54321
1-800-ISPYONU

Top Secret
This Letter Permitted to
Authorized Personnel Only

CONFIDENTIAL

Dear CodeCrusher:

We figured out that CodeMaker has a partner named Thomas Michaels. We snapped the picture below through a mirror in his room. It's a picture of something he wrote on his wall. But the only problem is that it is written backwards because of the mirror. You can probably read it and solve the riddle if you read it through another mirror. Then circle the reference of the verse it is talking about on the sheet to the left. The answer should guide you to some useful information.

Good Luck,
Mr. SuperSneaky

THIS VERSE TALKS ABOUT YOUR MOM AND DAD
THIS VERSE TRIES TO KEEP US FROM DOING BAD
THIS VERSE HELPS US REMEMBER
TWO REMEMBER, THREE REMEMBER, FOUR, FIVE, SIX!
ADD ALL OF THOSE NUMBERS AND YOU CAN FIX
THE REFERENCE OF YOUR VERSE INTO THIS:

CHAPTER 7:

A Study on Apple Eyeballs (Just Kidding)

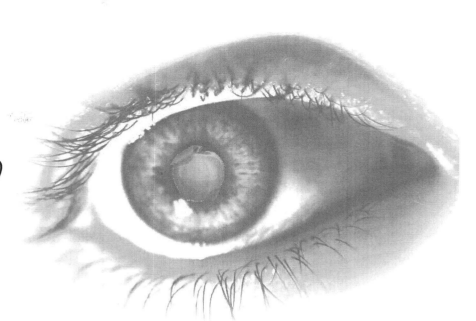

Go Read Proverbs 7:1-5

Proverbs 7! We're moving right along now. When the Bible repeats something over and over again, you had better pay close attention and listen to those words. Well, what is one common theme that we have seen over and over in Proverbs? We keep seeing the benefits of wisdom and the plea from Solomon and God to listen to wisdom, don't we? Let's look at the first couple verses of Proverbs 7. First of all what is the apple of your eye? No, you can't use it to make applesauce (Gross! Plus that would be called eye-plesauce). Well, there are two ways that you can read this. The first way to read this is that the apple of your eye is something very important to you. For example, your new titanium ultra-fast skating shoes might be considered the apple of your eye. The second apple of your eye is the part of your eyeball that allows you to see things. It's the very most important part of your eyeball. Anyway, look at how verse 2 tells us to PROTECT the teachings found in Proverbs like our eyeballs (or our favorite toy)! OK, have you ever played in a sand box when a little kid next to you started to throw sand in the air? Well, all that nasty dust got into your eyes. Then immediately your body started to wash the dust out. How? Your eyes started to water, right? Yep, your body was PROTECTING your eyeballs.

If you still don't think that you PROTECT your eyeballs super carefully, hold up two fingers and begin to move your hand toward your eyes as if you were going to poke yourself in the eyes. What is the first thing you do? You close your eyes, right? You don't even trust your own hands with your eyes. And what do you do if you find someone filling your new titanium ultra-fast skating shoes with MUD? You freak out, right?

Ok, what's the point? Well, you really, really want to PROTECT both of these things; they're both apples of your eye. You PROTECT the stuff that you love, like your eyeballs. Isn't it cool that Proverbs tells us to PROTECT the Proverbs and, really, the whole Bible like that? We're supposed to guard it with everything we have. Now, how do you PROTECT the stuff you learn in the Bible like your eyeballs? One thing you could do is make Bible-shaped glasses. Just kidding. What you *could* do is memorize the stuff you learn in the Bible. OK, breathe slowly; it's not that hard. Ask your parents to help you collect a few verses, and all you have to do is learn a verse a week. If your parents need help with that, they can visit our website. Anyway, according to Psalms (the big book before Proverbs), when you do that, you are hiding God's word in your heart. What better ways are there of PROTECTING something like you PROTECT your eyeball or skating shoes, than hiding it where no one can get to it, like in your heart?

Who Knew?

If you open up your Bible directly in the middle, you will probably end up in Psalms. And, if you really want to know, the middle chapter of the Bible is Psalm 118 and the middle verse is Psalm 118:8.

Quiz 18

1. What is the apple of *your* eye?

2. How are we supposed to guard the teachings in Proverbs according to Proverbs 7:2?

3. According to Psalms what are we supposed to do with God's Word? (Hint: Psalms 119:11)

4. What is one thing you learned from this section?

5. How are you going to apply what you learned today to your life?

Riddle Me This

Puzzle #1 – JUMBLED PHRASE

Divide the words with lines so that you can come up with a phrase. Like in the phrase, "Th isiss osi mple" Just put lines in so it says, "Th is|is| o|si mple." This is so simple, right?

wen eed togu ardt hesib le'ste ach ingsli

keth eap plea foure ye.

Go Read Proverbs 7:1-5 Again

Take a look at this weird verse:

> Say to wisdom, "You are my sister,"
> and to insight, "You are my relative." Proverbs 7:4 NIV

Ok, what does it mean to call wisdom your sister and understanding your relative?

Well, what are some things you know about your sister? That's a dumb question because you know a lot about her, don't you? For example, you know that she likes pizza, plays with ponies, and eats dirt. And you're probably very close to her. So when the Bible tells you to call wisdom your sister, it's telling us to work so hard on knowing wisdom that you end up knowing wisdom as well as you know your sister. And the relative thingy? Well, a relative is a family member, so it's telling us to do the same thing with understanding. How do we actually do this? Again, memorizing verses is a really useful tool. You could also pray over the things that you have learned. This just lets you talk to God about these things, and gives you a chance to ask Him to help you make this stuff stick in your head.

Study Up!

Memorize Psalm 119:11 to apply what we learned yesterday about guarding wisdom in our hearts!

Psalm 119:11

I have hidden Your word in my heart that I might not sin against You. (NIV)

Go Read Proverbs 7:6-27

Ok, as I've been saying, some stuff in Proverbs is for when you are older. Luckily, this is the last large portion we'll have to skip in Proverbs because of that adult stuff. The only reason I'm having you read it is so that you can tell all your friends, "Hey, I read through the whole book of Proverbs." Plus, it's a good habit to read everything in the Bible, not just the stuff you like the most.

Quiz 19

1. What does Proverbs mean when it talks about wisdom being your sister and understanding your relative?

2. How do you get closer to understanding and wisdom? (Hint: A good way is to memorize *something...*)

3. Why do you read all of the adult stuff even though it doesn't really apply to you right now?

4. What is one thing you learned from this section?

5. How are you going to apply what you learned today to your life?

Verse of **Fame**

__Proverbs 7:1__

My son, keep my words and store up my commands within you.

Puzzle #3– *Code Crusher*

Decoding directions contained in the letter… (just read the letter below)

Dear CodeCrusher:

Okey dokey, so, we found this word search in CodeMaker's bedroom. I hope it's useful. A note on CodeMaker's bed stand said that the words that are missing are hidden in the word search. So we had our keenest eyes find all of the words hidden within. Can you find them in the puzzle again? Do that before reading more…

Ok, some of the words that you found fit in the blanks, but not all of them. The answer should make up the start of a verse. If you get stuck the verse is Proverbs 7:4 (on page 66). Hope you can get it!

> Good Luck,
>   Mr. SuperSneaky

APPLE	SOLOMON
EYEBALL	WISDOM
SISTER	YOU

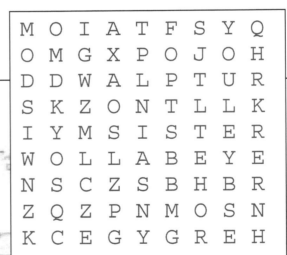

```
M O I A T F S Y Q
O M G X P O J O H
D D W A L P T U R
S K Z O N T L L K
I Y M S I S T E R
W O L L A B E Y E
N S C Z S B H B R
Z Q Z P N M O S N
K C E G Y G R E H
```

S a y   t o   _ _ _ _ _ _ _ , "_ _ _

a r e   m y   _ _ _ _ _ _ ."

CHAPTER 8:

CAN YOU HEAR ME NOW?!

Go Read Proverbs 8:1-11

Hey! Remember me for later!

GUESS who we get to listen to some more? Wisdom, and she is on a roll! This time, instead of threatening those who don't listen to her, she is pleading for people to listen up. Remember that whenever you read Proverbs, it is helpful to think of a picture in your head. The first verses of Chapter 8 talk about where wisdom is standing. Now, is wisdom a real life person, whose voice we can really hear? We all know that she isn't. So why does Proverbs tell us where she is standing? This is a trick that some writers use called personification, which takes something that's not alive and compares it to a person or some other living object. So, wisdom is not a real human being (which we already knew). You might be thinking of a very good question, but I'm going to ask it before you do. If wisdom is not a real person, then why does Proverbs take so much time to describe where wisdom is standing? Well, here is the thing. What this picture is showing you is that everybody has the chance to either accept or reject wisdom. God has placed wisdom in front of all people and has given them the opportunity to either reject it or accept it. He does the same

Who Knew?

Personification is a style of writing where you compare something that is not alive to something that is. For example the phrase, "The wind nipped at our coats." *Obviously*, the wind can't actually nip or bite like a dog. It's just showing how it's *like* a dog.

thing with Jesus. The Bible says that every single person (yes, every single person) has the opportunity to either know Him or reject Him.

In verse five, wisdom talks about what you can get from her (which we have already looked at). Why does she talk about what she says so much? She says that her words are, worthy, right and just. (NIV) Why? Well, because to those who listen to wisdom, the things that we learn from wisdom are worthy, right, just, and true.

Finally, brothers and sisters, whatever is true, whatever is noble, whatever is right, whatever is pure, whatever is lovely, whatever is admirable—if anything is excellent or praiseworthy—think about such things. Philippians 4:8 NIV

Ok, do you notice anything in COMMON between this verse and what wisdom says? This verse mentions some of the things that wisdom *is*, such as "right" and "worthy" (praiseworthy means worthy of praise). It gives us a really good reason for listening to wisdom, along with all of the other reasons that we have already seen.

Quiz 20

1. What is wisdom pleading us to do in this section? (Pssst! Look in the first three sentences of this chapter or you can look in Proverbs 8:4-6.)

2. What are some of the things that wisdom says she has? If you don't remember, you were obviously ASLEEP! (You can look back at Proverbs 8:5.)

3. Based on this chapter what do Philippians 4:8 and wisdom have in common?

4. What is one thing you learned from this section?

5. How are you going to apply what you learned today to your life?

Riddle Me This...

Puzzle #1 – **DOT** DELIRIUM

Did you notice all the little **DOTS** earlier in the text? (Yeah, like that one in the star that told you to "remember me for later"?) Don't expect them to be big dots; they look like this: • Start at the beginning (page 69) and look back through the first part of this chapter. Write down the letters that have a **DOT** over them in the order that you see them. In the end, you will complete another wise phrase.

P.S. – The first dot is actually in the star. It also has an arrow pointing to the letter it's over.

You who are __ __ __ __ __ __, gain prudence.

Go Read Proverbs 8:12-31

Ok, let's take a look at verses 14-17. Remember: Ms. Wisdom is still speaking.

> *I have good sense and advice, and I have understanding and power. I help kings to govern and rulers to make fair laws. Princes use me to lead, and so do all important people who judge fairly. I love those who love me, and those who seek me find me.*
> *Proverbs 8:14-17 NCV*

Who is the most important person you know? You might say someone like the governor of Maine, the police chief of San Francisco, or the President of the United States of America. OK, what is something that all these guys have in COMMON? (Hint: the answer is not that they all breathe air). These people all hold positions of power. Now, what do you think we should expect from these people? Do we expect bad choices that ruin the country or good decisions that strengthen our country? Of course, we expect good and wise decisions from these leaders, right? Well, these people need wisdom. And here is a little secret for you: you can have the same wisdom that these men need to rule a country. Isn't that cool? You don't have to be a super smart genius to rule a country (although it's helpful).

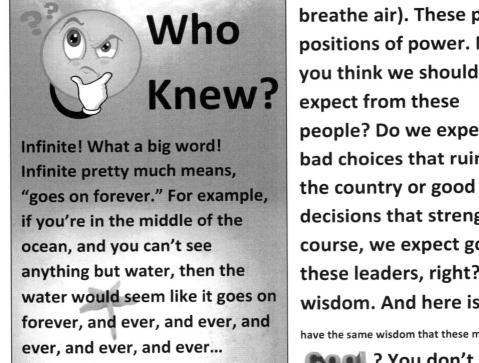

Who Knew?

Infinite! What a big word! Infinite pretty much means, "goes on forever." For example, if you're in the middle of the ocean, and you can't see anything but water, then the water would seem like it goes on forever, and ever, and ever, and ever, and ever, and ever… That's infinite!

Maine

You just have to be wise. Now one more quick thing. Get a load of verse 17.

> *"I love all who love me. Those who search will surely find me. Proverbs 8:17 NLT*

What is that saying? Let me ask you a question. How easy is it to find wisdom? I mean, according to that verse, how easy is it? OK, think about this... don't skip ahead and look at the answer. (There's a test at the end of this.) It seems like all you have to do is seek for wisdom and BAM! you're there. Funny, that's how God says it is with Him. He says:

> *"You will seek Me and find Me when you search for Me with all your heart."*
> *Jeremiah 29:13 NASB*

Hmm... It kind of seems that there are a lot of similar passages about God and wisdom... in fact, it seems like when you are looking for wisdom, you find yourself actually looking for God. It's the same way with finding wisdom – when you find wisdom, you find God.

Notice how wisdom was right there with God when He created everything. There are two things that you need to remember - #1: God is infinitely wise. I think we humans with our dumbo brains constantly DOUBT God's wisdom. We think, "AH! God, you have no idea what you're doing in this situation." We're so quick to DOUBT God's wisdom and His goodness. But it's almost as if wisdom shakes her finger at us and says, "No, trust me; He's wise." #2: We have access to God's wisdom, because it seems like that's the only type of wisdom that there is. So when you're wise, it's like you've gained a little piece of God's understanding. cool, huh?

Quiz 21

1. What is the only thing we need to do to get wisdom? (Hint: The answer is in verse 17.)

2. What does infinite mean?

3. What are two things we are supposed to notice in the last part of this section?

4. What is one thing you learned from this section?

5. How are you going to apply what you learned today to your life?

Riddle Me This...

Puzzle #2 – ANAGRAM MASTER

Unscramble this foolish phrase and put it back into a wise saying.
(Hint: Capital letters start each word.)

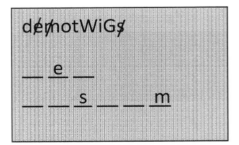

demotWiGs

__ e __ __

__ __ s __ __ m

Go Read Proverbs 8:32-36

Again, these are just the benefits of wisdom. There's something cool in verse 34. What exactly does this verse mean? What does it mean to watch at somebody's doorway every day? Well, have you ever been at the park and an ice cream truck rumbles up

> Blessed is the one who listens to me, watching daily at my gates, waiting beside my doors.
> Proverbs 8:34 ESV

BLARING the "Popeye the Sailor Man" theme song? (That's the weirdest ice cream eating song; unless you're eating spinach-flavored ice cream!) Have you ever noticed that the ice cream truck seems to come almost at the same time every day? Some kids at the park even wait for that time when the ice cream man comes so that they can be the first ones to get ice cream. Well, that's how we should act toward wisdom; we should be waiting for her to come out and give us wisdom. Since wisdom doesn't really have a house, you just need to pray that God will give you wisdom. Also, when you read the Bible every day, you are positioning yourself at wisdom's gates! Cool, huh?

Verse of Fame

Proverbs 8:10-11

Choose my instruction instead of silver, knowledge rather than choice gold, for wisdom is more precious than rubies, and nothing you desire can compare with her.

75

Quiz 22

1. In your own words, what does it mean to be watching someone's doorway every day? (Think "Popeye the Sailor Man" and ice cream.)

2. Name a couple of things that you always expect. Do you expect wisdom to come like you expect the other things to come?

3. What do we need to pray that God will give us?

4. What is one thing you learned from this section?

5. How are you going to apply what you learned today to your life?

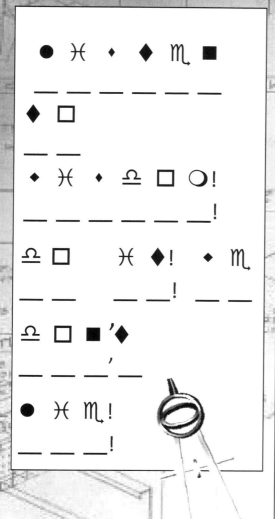

SuperSpiesRUs.INC   Top Secret
321 SuperSneak Ln.   This Letter Permitted to
Hidden, Hiding 54321   Authorized Personnel Only
1-800-ISPYONU

CONFIDENTIAL

Dear CodeCrusher:

My team of top secret spies managed to break into WeGotTheSecret.INC's headquarters, and we picked up the enclosed cipher ("si-fur" - something that helps you crack a code). It's kind of small, but, hey, beggars can't be choosers. Plus, what do you want me to do, return it and say, "Um, could you make this longer? It's a little, um... little." Anyway, WidGeTS says that this is their secret to success, but I wonder if they're lying. Maybe they'll tell you whether or not they lie. Yeah, right! Of course they won't! Why would they do that? Just switch the symbols to letters on the slip of paper you found using the cipher, and you should get the answer. That might help, but now, it's up to you, CodeCrusher.

      Good Luck,
          Mr. SuperSneaky

Top Secret:
Do not give to any
SuperSpy agent.
Authorized Personnel Only

D	E	I	L	M	N	O	S	T	W
♎	♏	♓	●	◯	■	□	•	◆	⬩

CHAPTER 9: TODAY'S GAME:

Wisdom vs. Foolishness

Go Read Proverbs 9:1-12

Ok, today Ms. Wisdom and Lady Foolishness get into a fight over souls. Now, we know that Ms. Wisdom is too wise to get into a foolish argument, but when you're dealing with someone's soul, you need to do whatever it takes. Let's see who wins. The first contestant to take the microphone is Ms. Wisdom. Now I know that we have heard a lot from her already, but we're going to continue to take a look at what she has to say, because review is the key to being successful at remembering important things (and no, I didn't make that up. Ask your teachers, parents or pastors; they'll tell you the same thing). OK, first of all, NOTICE that Ms. Wisdom is in a high place again. She is definitely in a place where she can be heard. It's also interesting that she makes her place attractive. She's basically being a really good commercial. Have you ever noticed that the things in commercials are often very brightly colored, never broken, and always work exactly right? Well, that's kind of what Ms. Wisdom is doing. She's promising that things will go well for people who listen to her. The only difference between Ms. Wisdom and a commercial is that we know that Ms. Wisdom isn't lying, like those commercials often do.

78

Quiz 23

1. Why does Ms. Wisdom get into a fight with Lady Foolishness? What are they fighting over?

2. What is Ms. Wisdom promising those who follow her?

3. What is Ms. Wisdom doing to her  ? Why?

4. What is one thing you learned from this section?

5. How are you going to apply what you learned today to your life?

Verse of Fame

Proverbs 9:10

The fear of the LORD is the beginning of wisdom, and knowledge of the Holy One is understanding.

Riddle Me This

<u>Puzzle #1</u> – **matchmaker**

Match the characteristic to the correct contestant. If you haven't already figured it out, both contestants have more than one characteristic, and both might share the same characteristic. Although, you should use a pencil; you might have to come back and make some corrections, because you'll learn more about these two ladies in the next sections.

Ms. Wisdom •

Lady Foolishness •

- TRIES **to make her home** ATTRACTIVE

- **Is in the** HIGH **place**

- **Offers things that are** TRUE

- **Is** UNATTRACTIVE

- LIES **and says that she is** good

- **Calls to the** simple

- EVERYONE **can hear her** voice

Go Read Proverbs 9:1-12 Again

According to Proverbs, who is Ms. Wisdom calling out to? She is calling to all the simple minded people (or the dumb people). Remember this little fact, because it will play a very interesting part a bit later on. Let's take a quick look at verses 7-9:

> *Anyone who rebukes a mocker will get an insult in return. Anyone who corrects the wicked will get hurt. So don't bother correcting mockers; they will only hate you. But correct the wise, and they will love you. Instruct the wise, and they will be even wiser. Teach the righteous, and they will learn even more. Proverbs 9:7-9 NLT*

What does verse 7 really mean? Well, let's come up with a picture that will help us understand. You know those kids at school who make fun of everyone? (If you're homeschooled, just play along.) OK, so imagine that during recess, those kids are making fun of Earnest Wilbur Eisenhower, the biggest nerd in the state of Maine. So you've read about this situation in every single Christian devotional out there; you're supposed to stand up for him, right? Well, what if you *don't*? You feel guilty, right? So let's say that you let them duct tape him to the flagpole. So, to ease your conscience, you approach them later after school (all alone) in a dark alley. You walk up to their leader, Bruno Bruiser, who is twirling a roll of duct tape on his finger. He grabs you by the shirt, lifts you twenty feet up into the air, and says, "Ooh, what do ya want, Puny?"

"Uh, Bruno, it, uh, might not be a good idea to, uh, duct tape nerds to flagpoles," you suggest.

Bruno looks kind of guilty and says, "You really think so? Oh man, I feel terrible. I'll never do it again."

Yeah right! He's going to go stick you up there right up next to poor Earnest, who's been there since recess; and he's going to leave you both there until you're eighty-seven years old.

Ok, why did I tell you such a terrifying story? Well, look at verse seven. It says that if you rebuke a mocker (or a teaser), you're only going to end up with trouble. Now there is a time to do what is right, but standing up is a lot different than a rebuke. When you stand up, you do it for yourself, or because it is the right thing to do. You can stand up for God, your beliefs, or even for a friend. When you stand up in your faith, you are strengthening your faith by stating your beliefs. But, when you rebuke someone, you are making a decision to approach them with some input. Why would you do that? So that you can bless them by helping them grow in an area they are weak in. Remember, rebuking someone is when you're trying to better *them*, and standing up for something that is right is something that is good for *you*.

Rebuke means to reprove. What's reprove? Well, it's telling someone that they're doing (or did) something wrong.

Unfortunately, mockers don't want any input from you. Now, if you would have said to Bruno, "Dude, leave him alone! That's not right!" *before* he tied up poor Earnest, that would have been a lot better than rebuking Bruno after school. In that situation, you would have been standing up for Earnest instead of rebuking Bruno. Either way, Bruno probably wouldn't have listened, because he's a mocker. On the other hand, a wise man will take correction, because he knows that if he follows it, he will only better himself. We'll take a closer look at how a wise person is teachable in later chapters.

For now, let's meet our second contestant, Lady Foolishness. OK, what are some things that we can see about Lady Foolishness? Think about these questions as you read the next section. Where is she? What does she do to make herself as attractive as Ms. Wisdom? Who is she calling to?

Quiz 24

1. What does Proverbs 9:7 mean?

2. What is the difference between standing up for your faith and rebuking a mocker?

3. Instead of rebuking Bruno after school, what would have been a better thing to do?

4. What is one thing you learned from this section?

5. How are you going to apply what you learned today to your life?

Riddle Me This

Puzzle #2 – RЄ + 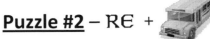 RAGE

Here's a rebus for you! (Rebus is a fancy word for picture math.) Have fun!

P. S. – in this puzzle, if you happen to come across a picture with certain spelling written on the *box*, use that spelling.

 -

__ __

 - k

__ __ __

(Rebus-us) + (duke-d)

__ __ __ __ __ __

a   __ __ __ __ __ __
__

Go Read Proverbs 9:13-18

Let's take a look at Lady Foolishness. Well, to begin, we see that she is in the highest part of the city. Wait a second! Who else is there? Well, we already know that is where Ms. Wisdom hangs out. So what does that mean about Lady Foolishness's voice? Everyone can hear her voice too, right? Just as everyone has a choice to either accept Wisdom and God's way, they also have the choice to reject Wisdom and choose Foolishness. You also need to see that you can't just choose to not choose. You always choose either Wisdom or Foolishness.

OK, let's move on. What does Lady Foolishness do to make herself ATTRACTIVE to those who pass by? OK, this is a deep question. Think about this carefully. What does she do? Absolutely nothing! She just sits there! Why? She doesn't even try because there is nothing ATTRACTIVE about foolishness. It's just pain and death. Now it's time for our last question. Who is she calling out to? She's calling out to the simple! This is interesting. The wise, those who fear the Lord, can't be simple anymore. So the people that Ms. Wisdom and Lady Foolishness fight over are the people who are simple. Now they might have not chosen Foolishness yet, but if they never choose Ms. Wisdom, then they AUTOMATICALLY choose Lady Foolishness.

Real Life

Make choices today that show others that you have let wisdom, and ultimately God, rule in your soul, and that foolishness has no control over you. Show others that wisdom is the right choice.

The same thing is said for Christians. Remember that Lady Foolishness and Ms. Wisdom are in a fight. They are fighting over souls, just like God and Satan are in a battle for souls. The cool thing is that God has already won in the Christian's life. There is still a battle, but in the end, God will win. Once you're a Christian, you're always a Christian, even if you mess up. Jesus has paid for all your sins. By

choosing Jesus and choosing to follow Jesus, you are also choosing the path of Wisdom. Let me ask you one more question. Have you **chosen** to follow Jesus and to be wise? If you haven't chosen Jesus, go find your mom and dad or your pastor, and ask them how you can know for sure that you have chosen Jesus, once and for all. Let me tell you, it will be the best thing that you will ever do. But, if your parents aren't available, you can also flip to page 296 of this book, and you'll find the answers that you're looking for.

Quiz 25

1. Why does Ms. Wisdom call out to the simple minded people? Why does Lady Foolishness call out to the simple minded people?

2. Where are both Lady Foolishness and Ms. Wisdom standing?

3. Why doesn't Lady Foolishness try to make herself attractive?

4. What is one thing you learned from this section?

5. How are you going to apply what you learned today to your life?

Puzzle #3- Code Crusher

Decoding directions contained in the letter... (just read the letter below)

11 = A

6 = D

10 = E

25 = F

23 = H

7 = I

22 = L

9 = N

5 = O

18 = S

21 = T

[N] [E] [<]

SuperSpiesRUs.INC
321 SuperSneak Ln.
Hidden, Hiding 54321
1-800-ISPYONU

Top Secret
This Letter Permitted to
Authorized Personnel Only

CONFIDENTIAL

Dear CodeCrusher:

We were flipping through CodeMaker's private folders, and this ribbon and piece of paper fell out. The paper was puzzling to us, and on the back of it, someone had written the words "valuable warning." We figured that the cipher was on the ribbon, so we took a look at it. Astonishingly enough, it was blank. The only thing it had written on it was that little NE< on the bottom. CodeCrusher, to find the cipher, try turning the ribbon northeast, but more towards the north. Something might come up, because when our chemist dusted it, he found that there was the slightest trace of a magnetic field-affected ink. Then you might know what to do.

> Good Luck,
> Mr. SuperSneaky

___ ___ ___ ___ ___ ___ ___ ___ ___ ___ ___ ___   ___ ___ ___ ___ ___   ___ ___   ___ ___ ___ ___ ___
25 5   5 22 7 18 23 9 10 18 18   22 10 11 6 18   21 5   6 10 11 21 23

CHAPTER 10:
WATCH YO' MOUTH, KID!

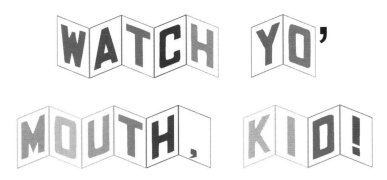

Go Read Proverbs 10

We need to take a different approach to our study of Proverbs, because from here on out, the rest of Proverbs is just a collection of different sayings. The first nine chapters of Proverbs had different main themes for each chapter, and that section of the chapter would stick closely to that theme. Unfortunately, no good thing lasts forever, right? So you're on your own from now on. Good luck!

No. Just kidding. We are still going to be looking at the main themes of the chapters; they just won't be so nicely grouped together. So let's jump into this. One of the things that you'll see over and over throughout Proverbs is to watch your speech. Here is where we are introduced to another character of Proverbs:

BAD IDEA

Don't stop reading Proverbs because it just got different. Keep reading; you never know what you'll find. Who knew - I mean - *knows*, you just might like the second part of Proverbs better than the first!

the chattering fool. Other names of this character include (but are not limited to): a blabber mouth, a gossip, a loudmouth, and someone who can stick their entire foot into their mouth.

Actually we'll take a much closer look at gossips, but for right now, let's take a look at the chattering fool found in Proverbs 10:8 and 10:10. Let's look at verse 8 first:

> *"The wise in heart will receive commandments: but a prating [chattering] fool shall fall." Proverbs 10:8 KJV*

This is that comparison thingy again. But doesn't it seem like the two things being compared don't quite match? Remember that a comparison is like taking two opposite things and looking at the things that make them different. So what's the wise in heart, who accept commands, have to do with a chattering fool? I mean, it seems like they are different, but not completely opposite.

Have you ever talked to someone who won't listen to a word you're saying because they're too busy telling you their own stories? Well, that is a chattering fool, someone who won't stop talking. When you go to tell them that they have an issue in their lives, are they going to be quiet while you tell them about it? Probably not. They will be too busy talking about other things. So Proverbs tells us that those who accept commands are wise, and a chattering fool comes to ruin. Make sense?

Quiz 26

1. Give several other names for the chattering fool.

2. What two things does this chapter compare?

3. What is one difference between your two answers from the last question?

4. What is one thing you learned from this section?

5. How are you going to apply what you learned today to your life?

Riddle Me This...

<u>Puzzle #1</u> – *Poetic* PUZZLER

Read this poem out loud to a parent and circle the reference of the mystery verse.

This verse tells us to watch our mouth
By using a weird contradiction to show us how
It says that the wise in heart accept rules
But those who chatter are complete fools
Please take this verse's message to heart
And stop chattering (for just a start)

- **Proverbs 10:2**

- **Proverbs 10:8**

- **Proverbs 10:12**

- **Proverbs 10:14**

Verse of Fame

<u>Proverbs 10:20</u>

The tongue of the righteous is choice silver, but the heart of the wicked is of little value.

Take a Closer Look at: Speech
(Go Read Proverbs 10 Again)

Let me explain this new title. We're going to use a "Closer Look" every time we introduce a new topic. In these sections, we'll focus on verses that specifically deal with the topic mentioned in the title.

This brings us to our next topic. Believe it or not, our speech is extremely

important, especially to God. Proverbs has a lot to say on speech. One thing that you should note is the comparisons. (There's that word again. If you don't remember it, go back and look in Chapter 3. We'll start to see it a lot more in the rest of the book.) But the things that are being compared in Chapter 10 are the righteous and the wicked, and, more specifically, what they say. What are some of the things that you notice about what the righteous say? Fill in this chart so that you can remember these things.

Verse:	The righteous tongue:
Proverbs 10:11	a fountain of life
Proverbs 10:20	
Proverbs 10:21	
Proverbs 10:31	
Proverbs 10:32	

Is that what you want your tongue to be? That would be pretty cool, wouldn't it? What does it mean that the tongue of the wise "feed many" (KJV) in verse 21? Like, do people actually take bites out of your tongue? Obviously not; that would be disgusting! So, what does it mean? It means that your tongue shouldn't harm them. The NLT says that the tongue of the righteous encourages many. Encouraging someone really lifts their spirits, doesn't it? Imagine that you were just yelled at by your music teacher and you are really sad because he really, really hurt your feelings. But then your friend is like, "Dude, you rock that tuba! I wish I could play like that!" How would you feel?

If you're still confused, take a close look at what Ephesians 4:29 says:

> *Do not let any unwholesome talk come out of your mouths, but only what is helpful for building others up according to their needs, that it may benefit those who listen. Ephesians 4:29 NIV*

Real Life

Say something nice to a friend today to make them feel loved and special.

What does unwholesome mean? Well, it means harmful or corrupt. So, what does "not letting any harmful speech escape from your mouth" look like? It means watch what you say. As the last part of this verse says, just say things that help people. Instead of telling people that they tend to be loud and annoying, tell them what a good friend they are in times of trouble. Remember, your tongue can either tear down someone or build them up.

Quiz 27

1. What does Proverbs mean when it says that our tongues should feed many?

2. What does "unwholesome" mean?

3. What should we do *other than* tearing people down with our words?

4. What is one thing you learned from this section?

5. How are you going to apply what you learned today to your life?

Puzzle #2 – Code Crusher

Decoding directions contained in the letter... (just read the letter below)

SuperSpiesRUs.INC
321 SuperSneak Ln.
Hidden, Hiding 54321
1-800-ISPYONU

CONFIDENTIAL

Top Secret
This Letter Permitted to
Authorized Personnel Only

Dear CodeCrusher:

And... here you go. One of our good friends sent us this piece of paper, and we think that it is probably connected to WidGeTS. Although I can't solve it, I might be able to give you a hint. It looks like some of the ink bled off the circles and onto the envelope, which means two things. One, the ink is fresh, and two, the circles were drawn on after the words were printed – probably drawn in to highlight a word or letters.

Good Luck,
Mr. SuperSneaky

| Encourage |
| Tongue |
| Unwholesome |
| Comparison |
| Chattering |

Do not let any ___?___ talk come out of your mouths-
__ __ __ __ __ __ __ __ __ __

Something used to compare the righteous and the chattering

Fool (Hint: Think scales) - __ __ __ __ __ __ __ __

Something in your mouth that helps you make the *th* sound-
__ __ __ __ __ __

Our speech is supposed to ___?___ many (the NLT version of Proverbs 10:21) - __ __ __ __ __ __ __ __

The wise in heart accept commands, but a ___?___ fool comes to ruin (NIV) - __ __ __ __ __ __ __ __ __ __ __

We are supposed to guard our __ __ __ __ __ __

CHAPTER 11:

Accurate Weights Make for a Good Workout???

Go Read Proverbs 11

Proverbs 11! We are doing so well. We are about a third of the way through Proverbs. Now, let's focus on honesty. But first, let's do a quick review of what we have learned so far. Remember that the fear of the Lord is the beginning of wisdom. Remember that there are consequences for our actions. Remember that Proverbs is a book that takes a lot of time to tell us about the consequences of our actions. It also takes a lot of time to compare righteous and wicked choices. Always remember that. If you have a complete understanding of what's going to happen because of your choices, then you will be a lot more likely to make wise decisions.

Real Life

Make a right choice today and see what consequence comes – a good one or a bad one.

Take a Closer Look at: Honesty

Let's take a look at the very, very first verse of chapter 11.

What are weights? Are they those big heavy things that you see those giant super-strong men lifting on television? Yes, but we're not talking about those kind of weights. The weights that this verse is talking about are used to measure how heavy things are. They weigh stuff by balancing an object with an unknown weight against an object with a known weight. Here, let me illustrate. It's like a TEETER TOTTER. Say you put a boy named Gordon on one side of the teeter totter. Nobody knows how much Gordon weighs. Now Hank wants to play on the teeter totter, and you know that Hank is 50 pounds and Hank has a lot of brothers who are exactly the same weight that he is. So, you can figure out how much Gordon weighs. How? All you have to do is put Hank and all of his brothers on the TEETER TOTTER until the teeter totter is level with the ground. From there you can figure out how heavy Gordon is.

Who Knew?

Did you know that when someone says, "That seems even," they are referring to a scale? When the scales are even, it's fair. So when someone says "That seems even," it also means "That seems fair."

Back in the old days this is how they would figure out how much something weighed. They would carry around little TEETER TOTTERS, called balances, and an object that they knew the exact weight of (just like we knew the exact weight of Hank). That way they could figure out the weight of something that had an unknown weight (like Gordon). They would use this tool to buy things by figuring out how much gold or silver it would take to make the other side (the one with the known weight) go up so that both sides would be level (just like we did with Hank and Gordon). However, sometimes people would cheat! They would make the balance so that one side was a lot heavier than the other side. That would mean that it would take a lot more gold to tip the scale. That's what you call dishonest weights.

Now that we know what a weight is, what is this verse saying? Basically, it's saying that God loves it when we are honest. He doesn't want us to cheat anyone but He wants us to always deal honestly with everyone.

> *Honesty guides good people; dishonesty destroys treacherous people. Proverbs 11:3 NLT*

Honesty is extremely important to God. Why? When we are honest, we are showing that we are children of God. Plus look at the benefit of honesty. It will guide you on the right path. Sounds a bit like wisdom, doesn't it? Guess why. Because when you're being honest, you're being wise. COOL, huh?

Quiz 28

1. You will be more motivated to make wise decisions if you ___?___.

2. How is cheating like dishonest scales?

3. Why is honesty important to God?

4. What is one thing you learned from this section?

5. How are you going to apply what you learned today to your life?

Riddle Me This...

Puzzle #1 – CaPiTaL CrAzY

Notice anything odd about the words below? If you take all of the capital letters (yes, ALL of them) and write them in the blanks below, you will come up with a wise phrase.

> Without a doubt, bEing an AmbassadoR would bE really cool. See? yoU would be able to ProPel airplanes acrOsS ocEans, cross DeserTs in trains, Or on a camel's Back. Everybody knows that you would wAnt to take your caMera so that you could get lots of pictures to send BAck home to your friendS and family, who miSs you terribly. Anyone can be an ambassaDor. they Only must live Right, Speak For whO they stand foR, and their Cats Have to live at home alone. RidIng the ambaSsador train is Tough. will you take it?

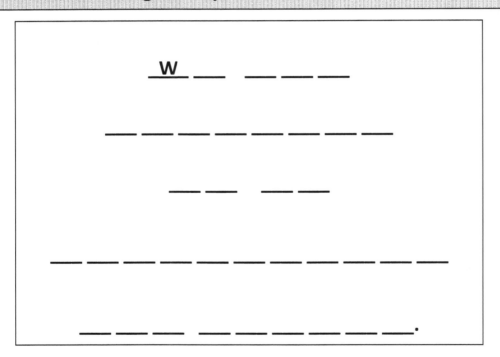

This puzzle will give you a sneak peek into what Chapter 12 is about!

Take a Closer Look at: *Generosity*

(Go Read Proverbs 11 Again)

What does *generosity* mean? And what is it? Well, *generosity* is the act of being generous. But what does it mean to be generous? Well, do you know someone who always seems to be giving stuff away? They always are giving people food, money, encouragement, or just about anything else. They are the type of people who give so much stuff away that you think that their house must be completely empty. Well, that is what a generous person is like. Let's take a look at verses 24-26:

> *Some people give much but get back even more. Others don't give what they should and end up poor. Whoever gives to others will get richer; those who help others will themselves be helped. People curse those who keep all the grain, but they bless the one who is willing to sell it. Proverbs 11:24-26 NCV*

What are some of the things that happen to the generous? First of all, they'll never run out of stuff, and they prosper (which means that they do well in their lives), and they are blessed. That goes against everything that we know, doesn't it? Don't we all know that when we give something away, it's gone and it will never come back? Yes, but what God tells us is that He will bless us even more.

Here is a saying that you should remember: You can't out-give God. Ok, let me explain this. You can outdo somebody, right? Like when you outrun somebody, it means that you run faster than them. Well, when you out-give someone, you are giving away more than they give away. You can't out-give God; He'll always beat you. (He's God, right?) Whenever you give something away, God will always give more back to you than you gave away. Now, it might not be in stuff, it might be something that you totally wouldn't expect. Here's one example, say you give someone some money that you really needed. God might provide you with the exact amount of money that you need. It has happened many times before. Also remember that God's timing might be different than ours, but He always will eventually bless you for being generous. And when He does, your generosity won't seem as much of a sacrifice any more. Now, I know that this kind of seems HARD and RISKY, but being generous is a good way to trust in God (we'll talk about that in a later chapter). Just know that everything that we have, we got from God. This allows us to be able to give our stuff to others, because it was all given to us anyway. When we give stuff away, we're blessing someone's life. We're just redistributing God's stuff. COOL, huh?

Verse
of
Fame

Proverbs 11:1

The LORD detests dishonest scales, but accurate weights find favor with him.

Definition:

Detest: Dislike intently (hate)

Quiz 29

1. Describe a *generous* person.

2. When you give a present to someone on their birthday, a lot of times they will, in turn, give you a present on *your* birthday. How is this a reward of being generous?

3. How does God tell us that He will reward a generous person?

4. What is one thing you learned from this section?

5. How are you going to apply what you learned today to your life?

ALWAYS REMEMBER:

If you give to others, you give to God, and God will give back to you.

Decoding directions contained in the letter… (just read the letter below)

SuperSpiesRUs.INC
321 SuperSneak Ln.
Hidden, Hiding 54321
1-800-ISPYONU

CONFIDENTIAL

Top Secret
This Letter Permitted to
Authorized Personnel Only

Dear CodeCrusher:

We found this ginormous magnetic message scroll right under CodeMaker's window. It probably fell out. I think you should try to find the words from the bottom right corner of this paper in the scroll. Then fill in the blanks below with the remaining letters that are not circled (going through each row horizontally).

Good Luck,
Mr. SuperSneaky

Generosity
Honesty
Scales
Weights
Fair

Y	H	O	U	C	A	W	N	N	E
V	O	E	R	G	E	I	V	E	M
O	N	R	E	I	T	H	A	N	G
O	E	D	G	S	C	A	L	E	S
H	S	H	A	S	G	I	V	E	N
Y	T	I	S	O	R	E	N	E	G
S	Y	Y	O	U	F	A	I	R	☺

___ ___ ___ ___ ___

___ ___ ___ ___ ___

___ ___ ___ ___ ___

___ ___ ___ ___ ___

___ ___ ___ ___ ___ ___

___ ___ ___ ___ ___ ___

___ ___ ___ .

CHAPTER 12:

Lazy Ambassadors? Ha!

Go Read Proverbs 12

I hope that you are still faithfully reading through Proverbs. If your goal is just to read this book instead of the Bible, just throw this book away. Nothing can compare with the Bible. Also, how cool would it be to tell your friends that you read through Proverbs and really understood it? It would be a huge blessing in your life.

Real Life

Before you start, pray and ask God to teach you something new and helpful about laziness.

Now, let's take a look at Chapter 12. By this time you should be noticing all of the similar themes in Proverbs. But remember that Proverbs is a book about consequences. All that Proverbs is doing is comparing the righteous and the wicked. It is looking at the consequences that come from making either righteous or wicked choices. We'll spend this chapter looking more at laziness.

Take a Closer Look at: Laziness

I know exactly what you are thinking. You're thinking something like, "This guy's lost it. We've already talked about laziness." Maybe I have lost it, but it seems like if the Bible repeats a whole bunch of topics, it is OK to take an extra look at some of those topics. So, we have already looked at the basics of laziness, so now we need to know why

being lazy is wrong. I mean, it seems like being lazy is fun, right? Who doesn't like to lie around and do nothing? But God has commanded us to be hard-working. Why? Well, first of all, laziness damages your reputation, and it damages God's reputation. OK, what is a reputation? Your reputation is one of the most valuable things that you have. Proverbs 22:1 says:

> *Choose a good reputation over great riches; being held in high esteem is better than silver or gold. Proverbs 22:1 NLT*

Are you ready to hear what a reputation is? Well, it's what people think of you. When you hear that someone doesn't do anything to HELP others, what do you think of that person? Your immediate reaction is to not want to hang around them at all. Why? Because you know that if you ever need HELP, that friend probably won't HELP you. Do you know this for sure? No, but that is what his reputation is. Does this make sense? Now, the cool thing about a reputation is that not only can you ruin it, but you can also build it up. When you make right choices that are honoring to God, you build a really good reputation for yourself.

Quiz 30

1. What is *your* definition of the word "reputation"?

2. Why is laziness dangerous to your reputation?

3. Pretend that you live in a town called Reputationville. Well, there's this guy named Joe Davis. He's a really nice guy and he loves to play basketball with you and all of the other neighborhood kids. But one day, he goes out and robs Reputationville's

bank. Soon, the sheriff is looking for him. Now you don't want to hang around him, right? So how should this story motivate you not to be like Joe Davis and to keep a good reputation?

4. What is one thing you learned from this section?

5. How are you going to apply what you learned today to your life?

Riddle Me This...

<u>Puzzle #1</u> – **matchmaker**

Proverbs 12 also compares the righteous and the wicked for a bit. Skim back through the chapter, and match the attribute to either "Righteous" or "Wicked".

Righteous •

Wicked •

- Choose their friends carefully

- Their ways lead them astray

- Words cause harm

- Care for the needs of their animals

- Cannot root itself somewhere

- Advice leads people astray

- Cannot be taken away

- Plans are just

- Their kindest acts are mean

- No harm overtakes them

- There is life on their path

- They have their full of trouble

Go Read Proverbs 12 Again

Take a look back at that example from the previous section. Do you see how *laziness* can affect your reputation? It doesn't make your reputation look very good, does it? Now, I realize that you are a long, long way off from having a job, but when you have a reputation for being lazy, you aren't very likely to keep your job for very long. Also, how does your *laziness* affect God's reputation? I mean, does your reputation affect your friends? It can, but not very much. What about your parents? Your reputation has a *huge* effect on your parents! Here let me give you an example. Whenever people see a dog do something that they know it shouldn't do, who do they blame: the dog or the owner of the dog? They most likely blame the owner. Why? Well, because it is the owner's job to teach their dog not to do certain things. People just assume that the owner has failed at her job of training her dog. The same thing could happen with you and God. When we become Christians, we become God's children. Therefore our actions reflect on God. This is how this whole thing looks:

WHOA! SOMEHTING IS *TOTALLY WRONG* HERE! JESUS SHOULDN'T BE REPRESENTED LIKE THAT!

Is that how you want to make Jesus look? We are supposed to give God a good name, and often, this doesn't happen. People sometimes say, "I don't want to follow God, because there is nothing different between Christians and regular people!" That's extremely sad. We aren't giving God a good name at all. We need to change this. One of the best ways that we can do this is to work hard in what we are given. If we are lazy, we are just being like the rest of the world. God's name can get insulted by our actions!

Quiz 31

1. How would your reputation affect your job if you had one?

2. How does your reputation affect your friends?

3. How does your reputation affect your parents?

4. What is one thing you learned from this section?

5. How are you going to apply what you learned today to your life?

Riddle Me This...

<u>**Puzzle #2**</u> – WORD CODE

Crack the code by using the cipher.

O z a r m v h h   t r e v h   b l f   z

_ _ _ _ _ _ _ _   _ _ _ _ _   _ _ _   _

y z w   i v k f g z g r l m

_ _ _   _ _ _ _ _ _ _ _ _ _

Verse
of
Fame

<u>Proverbs 12:25</u>

Anxiety weighs down the heart, but a kind word cheers it up.

A = Z	N = M
B = Y	O = L
C = X	P = K
D = W	Q = J
E = V	R = I
F = U	S = H
G = T	T = G
H = S	U = F
I = R	V = E
J = Q	W = D
K = P	X = C
L = O	Y = B
M = N	Z = A

Go Read Proverbs 12 (yes, *again*)

OK, check out this verse from 2 Corinthians:

> Therefore, we are ambassadors for Christ,
> as though God were making an appeal through us;
> we beg you on behalf of Christ, be reconciled to God.
> 2 Corinthians 5:20 NASB

What on earth is an ambassador? An ambassador represents a country. Sometimes, different countries get into an argument. When this happens, each country sends a person to the other country. This person then talks to the other country about the interests of their home country. Now, why does God call us His ambassadors? Well, because we represent His country. Philippians 3:20 says:

> But we are citizens of heaven, where the Lord Jesus Christ lives.
> And we are eagerly waiting for Him to return as our Savior.
> Philippians 3:20 NLT

A citizen is someone who is part of a country, whether they like it or not. The Bible calls us citizens of God's country! How cool is that? But with that, there comes a great responsibility. We are to be His ambassadors in this world. We must be good ambassadors so that God will have a good reputation. cool,  huh? Your good reputation = God's good reputation! They aren't separate! They go hand in hand!

Quiz 32

1. What is an ambassador?

2. Ambassadors represent a country. Who do we represent?

3. Let's say that a little girl threw an eraser at her teacher because she got an F on her test. After that, nobody wanted to hang around her because they didn't want her to throw things at *them* whenever she got mad. How did her actions hurt her reputation?

4. What is one thing you learned from this section?

5. How are you going to apply what you learned today to your life?

Puzzle #3- *Code Crusher*

Decoding directions contained in the letter... (just read the letter below)

Dear CodeCrusher:

We were looking for some new information from WeGotTheSecret.INC, when we found a couple more magnetic scrolls. It looks like he programmed in several letters. But, on one of the handles, we found writing which said, "Not safe. Insert spaces." So try drawing lines between the words. You might find a useful phrase...

Good Luck,
Mr. SuperSneaky

Rev iewisth ekey tosuc cess. Byt hew ayd on't for gett hatrig hteo usne ssag ainst wick edne ssiss catt eredth roug houtal lof Pr ove rbs.

Not safe. Insert spaces.

Write the encrypted message on the lines below.

_____
_____
_____
_____
_____
_____
_____
_____
_____
_____

CHAPTER 13: WICKED, WICKED MAN, YOU BRUTE!!!

Go Read Proverbs 13

Let's now look at the wicked man. What about the wicked man, you might ask? Well, his wickedness. Here we go. You may remember those questions in Chapter 4 that described the wicked man's path. If you don't, stop reading and go look at it again real quick. (It's on page 41.) If you still don't remember, you probably aren't reading the Bible either. This can't be repeated enough: read these chapters! Anyway, we'll learn a ton by studying the wicked man.

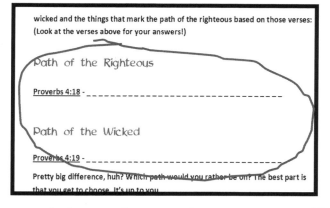

wicked and the things that mark the path of the righteous based on those verses: (Look at the verses above for your answers!)

Path of the Righteous

Proverbs 4:18 - _____

Path of the Wicked

Proverbs 4:19 - _____

Pretty big difference, huh? Which path would you rather be on? The best part is that you get to choose. It's up to you.

Take a Closer Look at: Wickedness

Based on what we saw in Chapter 4, what marks the path of the wicked? Darkness marks the wicked path, right? Honestly, this whole chapter gives amazing examples of that darkness. We'll take a look at what marks the wicked man a little later, but for right now, let's look at what makes a righteous man righteous:

> *The righteous hate what is false, but the wicked make themselves a stench and bring shame on themselves. Proverbs 13:5 NIV*

When you read this, notice that one phrase, "The righteous hate what is false." That sounds bad. In our lives, we all have something "false" that we don't really hate. This might be that TV show that you can't watch, that lie that you told, that cookie that you can't eat, or that game that you can't play. Wait a second! What is false about those things? Well, they promise you good things, but in the end, they land you in a bad place. Get this: the righteous HATE those things. Whatever came to your mind when you heard that phrase, "what is false"; the righteous HATE it! Kind of sounds dull and lame, doesn't it?

Seriously, do the righteous have any fun? Everybody must hate the righteous because they never have any fun, right? WRONG! Read this part of that verse again: "But the wicked make themselves a stench and bring shame on themselves." Did you get that? The wicked make themselves stink! How can this be? I mean, in our culture, everything that is bad seems like it is the coolest, smartest, and the funnest thing to do all the time. So what does it mean when it says that the wicked make themselves smell as bad as a skunk? Well, have

Real Life

When you are tempted to do something wrong today, instead of doing it, say "I hate this sin!" to yourself. It may help you to not give in to evil.

you ever hung out with people who always do what they want, never think about anyone else, and are often quick to betray their own friends? Nobody likes to hang out with these people, almost as if they smelled bad! What a different way to look at that! Now, you might say, "Oh, I can watch those TV shows and still be a good person."

Chances are that the reason you aren't allowed to watch that show is because it has a bad influence on you. You just need to trust your parents and that they know what they are doing. If you're influenced by bad influences, you will begin to stink – just like those influences. Now we all want to smell nice, but smelling nice might mean that you can't watch that TV show, eat that cookie, or play that video game. But at least you won't be this guy. Yuck! A stink bug!

Quiz 33

1. If "what is false" can also mean "what is wrong," then rewrite the phrase, "The righteous hate what is false."

2. Is the **funnest** choice always the best one? Why, or why not?

3. Remember Joe Davis (Page 105)? No one hung around him, almost as if he stank because he did what was wrong. How should this help us avoid "what is false"?

4. What is one thing you learned from this section?

5. How are you going to apply what you learned today to your life?

Riddle Me This...

<u>Puzzle #1</u> – *MAZE MAYHEM*

Wickedness leads you down the path that you don't want to follow. Help Jasmine follow the good path by helping her make the right choices. Can you lead Jasmine in the right direction? Watch out for evil along the way!

Go Read Proverbs 13 Again

The very next verse continues with this theme about the wicked:

> *Doing what is right protects the honest person, but doing evil ruins the sinner. Proverbs 13:6 NCV*

What does wickedness do to the wicked man? It misleads him, right? What does righteousness do to the righteous man? It protects his path, right? OK, let's imagine this: suppose you wanted to go on a safari to see weird AFRICAN animals. You get to AFRICA and are ready to go. However, the only thing that you need is a good compass. So (obviously) you go to the compass hut, where this little AFRICAN man is selling a lot of compasses. You look at two different compasses. One of the compasses sings a little song when you pick it up. Otherwise, it's absolutely worthless. The other one is plain (no little songs), but it is absolutely trustworthy. You only have enough money to buy one (nice try). Obviously, you buy the one that sings, go out on your safari, and disappear forever.

Remember, a false compass in a dangerous situation doesn't mean that you get your directions mixed up for five minutes. It means that you die. That's how important a good compass is.

This is what righteousness and wickedness are like. They are like two compasses. Wickedness is the compass that sings, and righteousness is the trustworthy one. Even though the wicked compass seems like it is a lot cooler, it will only lead you to destruction and death. But the righteous compass leads you exactly where you need to go, even though it is a bit plainer than the wicked compass.

Quiz 34

1. What does wickedness do to the wicked? What does righteousness do to the righteous?

2. The **fun** compass in the story was not the best compass. It misled. How is that like choices in real life?

3. Some things in life make you think that they are the best choice – like the compass that sang. It looked like the best choice, but it wasn't. What are some choices in your own life that looked like the best choice, but they definitely weren't?

4. What is one thing you learned from this section?

5. How are you going to apply what you learned today to your life?

Riddle Me This...

Puzzle #2 – RE + RAGE

You know the drill. Just do the picture math.

 (– t – h) + ked

_ _ _ _ _ _

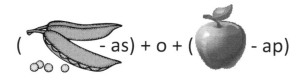 (– as) + o + (– ap)

_ _ _ _ _ _ _

M + ( – c)

_ _ _ _ _ _

Them + s +

_ _ _ _ _ _ _ _

St +

_ _ _ _ _

Verse
of
Fame

Proverbs 13:20

Walk with the wise and become wise, for a companion of fools suffers harm.

Go Read Proverbs 13 (yes, *again*)

Let's look at one more verse:

> *The life of the godly is full of light and joy, but the light of the wicked will be snuffed out. Proverbs 13:9 NLT*

OK, by now you should know that whatever snuffed out means, it is not good. Before I explain what snuffing stuff out means, you MAY NOT try this (at least until you're out of your parents' house). You did not learn it in this book, and I don't want to hear about any burns. OK, with that, let's take a look at FIRE. Fire, in order to burn, needs three things: fuel, air (oxygen), and heat. Whenever you cut out one of these three ingredients, your FIRE dies out. Now, let's say that you have a candle. If you take a glass and put it over the candle, it will go out, because the glass keeps all of the oxygen away from the flame. That's why if you pour water on FIRE, it goes out because the flame can't get oxygen. Now if you were to lick your fingers and quickly pinch the flame of the candle, it would go out, because your finger takes away the oxygen. This is what snuffing out a flame is. Let's look at the last part of that verse again. God is promising that He will pinch out the light of the wicked! However, in the first part, He says that He'll let the candle of the righteous burn brightly. If you're still tempted by that bad TV show, that video game, or that cookie, you should reread the three verses that we looked at in this chapter. This is serious stuff to think about.

BAD IDEA

Things that are tempting to you will quench out your flame. So avoid things that aren't helpful to you at all costs in order to keep your light shining.

Quiz 35

1. What is *your* definition of the phrase "snuffed out"?

2. Without oxygen, a light dies out. What are two things that you need in order to not be snuffed out?

3. What are some things you can do to keep your "spiritual light" from being snuffed out?

4. What is one thing you learned from this section?

5. How are you going to apply what you learned today to your life?

Puzzle #3 – Code Crusher

Decoding directions contained in the letter... (just read the letter below)

CONFIDENTIAL

Dear CodeCrusher:

Aaaugh! We were almost caught this time... again! We found the slip of paper below in Thomas Michaels's room. We also snapped this picture of a piece of paper off his desk. What I think that you should do is unscramble the words on the picture into a sentence. Then, unscramble the blocks into order so that it matches the sentence (some words will be split between multiple blocks). Well, I have to go do a little bit of research about Thomas Michaels.

Good Luck,
Mr. SuperSneaky

be lives of out
the the wicked
will snuffed

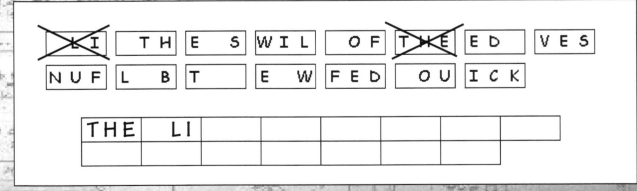

CHAPTER 14:

BEWARE! From here on out, Metal Man can change his shade of gray. He'll be harder to find!

Fools Will Be Fools

Go Read Proverbs 14

Today, we get to find out what a fool looks like. This may be frustrating at times because we might see some of these characteristics in our own lives. Then it can be easy to get mad because *someone* called you a fool. Well, Proverbs tells us that the way to stop being a fool is by listening to instruction. So let's read some instructions so that we don't become fools! Shall we?

BAD IDEA

When you come across an area in your life where you need to stop doing something, make a right choice instead of the bad choice. Instead of just trying to stop, have something good to do in place of the bad thing.

Take a Closer Look at: a Fool

Check out this verse:

A wise woman builds her home, but a foolish woman tears it down with her own hands. Proverbs 14:1 NLT

The whole chapter starts out with two women: the wise one and the foolish one. OK, what do we see the first woman doing? How about the second woman? Hold on. What? She's tearing down her HOUSE! That sounds like she might have a few brain problems. OK, let's take a closer look: does a foolish woman tearing down her HOUSE make any sense? Kind of, but not really.

OK, ladies, listen up; guys, hold up. This is talking about mothering and being a good wife. Now, I know that you're not thinking about having a husband for a long, long time, but what this section is talking about is good and bad womanhood. The wise woman makes good choices in her *marriage* and parenting. In doing this, she is building her home. Now, she's not literally building a house. But she is building her household and family with the good choices that she makes. The foolish woman is making bad choices in her marriage and parenting, which will lead to a wrecked home. In a sense, she is tearing down her HOUSEHOLD through the choices she makes.

OK, guys come back. This applies for you too. Make wise choices when you get a family of your own.

Quiz 36

1. When you get frustrated because you realize that some of the characteristics of a fool can be found in your life, you should remember that ___?___ can help you take those things out. (Hint: We've talked about this since day one.)

2. What, in your own words, does Proverbs mean when it talks about the woman who tears her house down? How does she tear her house down?

3. What are some things you can do to avoid "tearing down your house"?

4. What is one thing you learned from this section?

5. How are you going to apply what you learned today to your life?

Riddle Me This...

Puzzle #1 – *Poetic* PUZZLER
Read this poem out loud to a parent and circle the reference of the mystery verse.

This verse is warning us of tearing down our lives
By giving us the example of two wives.
One tore down her house with her own hands
But the wise woman's house alone still stands
Hear this lesson and learn it well
And notice how the foolish woman's house fell.

- Proverbs 14:1

- Proverbs 14:15

- Proverbs 14:23

- Proverbs 14:35

Go Read Proverbs 14 Again

Ok gang, check this out:

> "A fool's proud talk becomes a rod that beats him,
> but the words of the wise keep them safe." Proverbs 14:3 NLT

Wow! A fool's words become a rod that beats him! OK, let's look at this: obviously his words don't form a rod. So, what does it mean? Have you ever hung out with someone who brags all the time? Like Billy Winkerbean. You know that he's completely full of beans and that he can't really do all of that stuff that he claims that He can do. OK, I admit it; sometimes it is extremely fun to trap him in his lies. You might ask him something like, "Billy, are you sure you can fly a plane singlehandedly through the Grand Canyon blindfolded?" When he says, "Yes," kids, what is the next thing you always say? "PROVE IT!" You will probably hear something like, "Uh, peanut butter got caught in the control panel of my plane... and... uh... a dragon ate my blindfold." What did his lies do? They tangled him up. Chances are that if there were any of his friends there, they would start to call him Billy Peanut-Plane because of his lie. When you're made fun of like that, it's like getting beat with a stick. That's one of the ways a fool's words can become a stick that beats him. If you're not careful with what you say, you might get *trapped,* and everybody could start to make fun of your dumbness. But even worse, do you remember that God sees everything that we do? And do you remember that He has a response to everything that we do? Yep, God sees those little white lies too. Just don't lie or brag, because God will respond.

Anyway, what's that verse say that the words of the wise do? They protect them, right? When you're careful with what you say, your words will protect you. That's a pretty big difference. Foolish speech beats a man, but wise speech protects him. COOL, huh?

Quiz 37

1. Is it always okay to expose a liar (like asking Billy Winkerbean to prove his lie - is that always appropriate)?

2. How did Billy Winkerbean's words become a rod that beat him?

3. Thinking back to Billy Winkerbean, is telling half the truth the same as lying?

4. What is one thing you learned from this section?

5. How are you going to apply what you learned today to your life?

Verse
of
Fame

Proverbs 14:12

There is a way that appears to be right, but in the end it leads to death.

Riddle Me This...

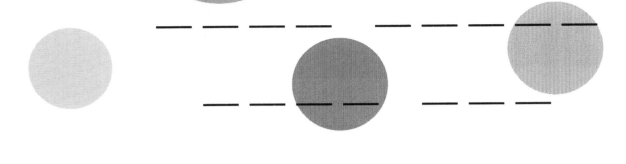

Puzzle #2 – DOT DELIRIUM

If you don't remember how to solve this puzzle, check out the first game in Chapter 8 (page 71).

__ __ __ __   __ __ __ __ __

__ __ __ __   __ __ __

__ __ __ __

Go Read Proverbs 14 (yes, *again*)

Ok, let's take a look at Proverbs 14:17:

> *A quick-tempered man acts foolishly,*
> *and a man of evil devices is hated. Proverbs 14:17 NASB*

What do you think that means? What does it mean to have a QUICk tEMPER? Have you ever had one of those days when you feel like you're a time bomb? It feels like anything could set you off and you could just **explode** because you're so angry. That is what being quick-tempered is. It means that you can get angry really, really quickly. Well, what does this verse say happens when you are QUICk tEMPERED? It says that a QUICk tEMPER will cause you to do foolish stuff. So I know that it is tempting to say, "Oh, I never do that!" But do you? What about when your little sister messes with your stuff? Or when your mom asks you to do something that you really, *really* don't want to do? How is your temper then? Let me share an interesting quote with you.

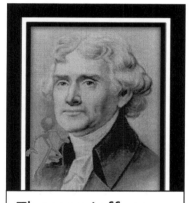

Thomas Jefferson

"When angry, count to ten before you speak. If very angry, count to one hundred." -Thomas Jefferson.

What was Jefferson saying? Well, whenever you become angry, it is a good idea to take a deep breath before you answer. That way, you can think through all of your words before you say them. He said count to ten, so that you have enough time and don't say anything that you will later regret. Check out this verse:

> *My dear brothers and sisters, take note of this: Everyone should be*
> *quick to listen, slow to speak and slow to become angry.*
> *James 1:19 NIV*

Be slow to speak. You'll save yourself a lot of bad consequences if you do that.

Look back up at Proverbs 14:17 (the first scroll on the last page). What is that last part of that verse saying? And what is an evil device? Well, an evil device is anything that can be used for hurting others. They can  range from a plan, a catapult, or even Brussels sprouts. Don't use those against other people. Look out for the best interests of others, and you will be honored and respected. That's all that the verse is saying.

Real Life

Whenever you are tempted to use an evil device, try to stay as far away from it as you can. Instead, bless people.

Quiz 38

1. What are some things that you can do to settle down your temper?

2. What does God want us to do with our anger?

3. What is an *EVIL* device?

4. What is one thing you learned from this section?

5. How are you going to apply what you learned today to your life?

Puzzle #3– Code Crusher

Decoding directions contained in the letter... (just read the letter below)

Dear CodeCrusher:

We were faxed this puzzle from one of our allies, SneakyThiefy's. It's another one of those crossword things. I think that some of the words didn't make it through the fax process on the second sheet – or maybe it was on purpose?

Good Luck,

Mr. SuperSneaky

Across

2. A quick tempered man acts _____.

3. An _____ _____ is anything that can be used for hurting others.

5. Everyone should be quick to listen, slow to _____ ...
(James 1:19)

6. "If very angry, count to ___ _____"

Down

1. You are studying the book of _____.

4. Thomas _____ said, "If angry, count to ten. If very angry, count to one hundred."

CHAPTER 15:

THE BLENDED REMOTES OF BENJAMIN FRANKLIN

Go Read Proverbs 15

Now, we get to look at the benefits of listening to... discipline (you thought I was going to say wisdom). Sometimes it can be so easy to think that we get disciplined unfairly. We **NEVER** deserve discipline in our own minds, do we? We either think that we always get it unfairly, or it never applies to us. God sees this very differently. Let's take a look at what He has to say about discipline.

Real Life

When someone corrects you today, say, "Okay. I'll try to work on not doing that," instead of complaining or whining about what they said.

Take a Closer Look at: Discipline

Remember that when we look at some of these topics, you might get annoyed because you realize that you are doing the wrong thing. Don't let that bog you down. Get back up, keep going, and learn from your mistakes. Let me ask you a question: how often do you get correction or discipline? You might hear stuff that sounds a lot like this: "Freddie, don't play on the roof… Freddie, don't cross your eyes or they'll stick like that… Freddie, don't sit too close to the TV… Freddie, don't stick the remotes in the blender…" It sometimes seems like you can't do anything **FUN**. Why do your parents tell you not to do that stuff? Is it because they want to be mean and not let you have the

childhood you deserve? We would all like to believe that, but we all know that it's not true. That is what Satan would like you to believe. He loves to WHISPER in your ear, "Your parents are just trying to be mean to you; they don't love you." However, the truth is that your parents do love you. But if they love us, why do they always take away our **FUN**?

They do it because they want what is best for us, nut just what is fun for us.

Quiz 39

1. Pretend that you are a young tree (just pretend – don't bury yourself!). Every once in a while, a gardener comes out and clips off some of your lower branches. You think that you've done *nothing* to deserve this horrid treatment. But in reality, if you clip a young tree's lower branches, it saves the tree a lot of energy and helps it grow up instead of out. How is this like discipline?

2. People always say, "Learn from your experiences!" What does that mean?

133

3. Why do our parents give us so many rules? (Say it in your own words. Like, you can't say "because they love me." Be creative.)

4. What is one thing you learned from this section?

5. How are you going to apply what you learned today to your life?

Riddle Me This...

Puzzle #1– JUMBLED PHRASE
Just put in lines to separate words in order to reveal a hidden message.
(Hint: You should have 25 words when you are done.)

SAT ANLI ESAN DSA YSTH ATYO URPA RENTS ARET RYI NGTO HUR TYOU .THE YLO VEY OUA NDTR YTO DOON LYWH ATISB ESTF ORY OU.

_____

_____

_____

_____

Go Read Proverbs 15 Again

Let's look at two really cool verses:

> Children, obey your parents in all things,
> because this pleases the Lord. Colossians 3:20 NCV
>
> Do everything without complaining or arguing. Philippians 2:14 NCV

Uh, oh! We're supposed to obey our parents? And we're supposed to do it without complaining or arguing? Oh boy! OK, it's not that bad. The Bible says:

> Fools reject their parents' correction, but anyone who accepts
> correction is wise. Proverbs 15:5 NCV
>
> If you listen to correction to improve your life,
> you will live among the wise. Proverbs 15:31 NCV

Your ears should perk at the mention of wisdom. What does that verse say? It says that whoever accepts correction is wise. What is accepting correction? It means that whenever someone tells you something to change about yourself, if you are wise, you will listen to them. What is the second verse saying? It is telling you that if you listen to correction, you will be considered wise. **WOW**! What does correction do (look at Proverbs 15:31)? _____

How can correction improve your life? Well, remember how earlier I said that your parents try and give you correction that is GOOD for you? Well, the same is true for everyone who gives you correction. They only give you correction to try to make you a better person. Sometimes you don't necessarily need the correction, but if you take it, you'll only better yourself. Benjamin Franklin said,

"WISE MEN DON'T NEED ADVICE. FOOLS WON'T TAKE IT."

OK, what is Ben saying? Wise men, even though they might not need correction, always take correction. A fool won't listen to correction, because they don't think that they need it.

Who Knew?

Did you know that Benjamin was so wise that he became an important leader in our country, and was known especially for his wisdom and discretion? That's pretty neat, isn't it?

Ben Franklin

Quiz 40

1. *How* are we supposed to obey our parents? (Look at Philippians 2:14 if you need help.)

2. How can correction help your life?

3. Why won't a fool listen to correction?

4. What is one thing you learned from this section?

5. How are you going to apply what you learned today to your life?

Riddle Me This...

Puzzle #2– Anagram Master

Solve the anagram by scrambling the words into a word that is closely related to today's reading of Proverbs

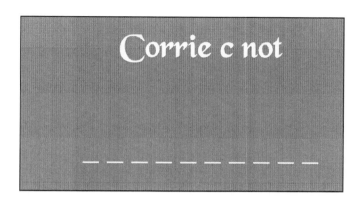

Corrie c not

_ _ _ _ _ _ _ _ _ _ _

Go Read Proverbs 15 (yes, *again*)

Let's take a look at verse 10:

> *Whoever abandons the right path will be severely disciplined; whoever hates correction will die. Proverbs 15:10 NLT*

What? Whoever hates correction will *die*! Does that seem harsh? Maybe... but maybe not. Here is a good story that I once heard that will help you understand this:

One time there was a little boy named **Stanley**. On his birthday, **Stanley** got a new puppy named Sparky. Now Stanley loved to play with Sparky and he liked to take him to the park. But his parents would always tell him, "Leave Sparky on his leash." Well, for a while, **Stanley** listened to his parents. **Stanley** and Sparky would have fun every single day at the park chasing squirrels and cats and just about everything else.

One day, after they had been playing at the park for a long time, **Stanley** thought to himself: "Wow. I bet Sparky would like being off his leash. It must choke him, and it is probably terribly uncomfortable. And he would sure get those squirrels a lot faster." So **Stanley** took off Sparky's leash. They had a great time and went home later that day. When **Stanley** got home, he told his parents about how much fun Sparky had off of his leash. But his dad told him: "Don't do that again **Stanley**. It's not safe for Sparky." But **Stanley** didn't listen. The next day, **Stanley** did the exact same thing. They had a lot of fun until Sparky ran out into the street and got hit by a car. Sparky died later that day, and **Stanley** learned a very valuable, but a very hard lesson.

138

I know that this is a very sad story. But it shows us something very important. Stanley didn't listen to his parents' correction, and he suffered greatly. When you listen to correction and accept discipline, you keep yourself from danger. If Stanley had only listened to his parents, things would have gone very differently for him and Sparky. But because he didn't take correction, Sparky died, and Stanley was left very sad and lonely. Even though it seemed mean to keep Sparky on his leash, it was the right thing to do. Sometimes correction may not make a lot of sense, but it will keep you out of harm's way. Is there something in your life that your parents have given you input on and you're not listening to correction? Pray for God to help you have a humble heart. He will be faithful to answer your prayer. Just remember that the Bible says that if you listen to correction and discipline, you will be wise!

Verse
of
Fame

Proverbs 15:1
A gentle answer turns away wrath, but a harsh word stirs up anger.

Quiz 41

1. What are some ways that ignoring correction can HURT you?

2. When you don't listen to your parents, are you the only one who can get HURT? (Read the Sparky story again if you need to.)

3. Now name a couple of ways ignoring correction can HURT others.

4. What is one thing you learned from this section?

5. How are you going to apply what you learned today to your life?

Puzzle #3– Code Crusher

Decoding directions contained in the letter... (just read the letter below)

Dear CodeCrusher:

I found this word search puzzle while I was looking up files about Thomas Michaels. I'm not quite sure what the second piece of paper is for, but I'm sure you can figure it out. Oh, and I also found the list of words below. What I think you should do is find the words, and then use the extra letters. It might be a useful phrase. It is all up to you now.

Good Luck,
Mr. SuperSneaky

L	I	S	T	E	T	N	T	H	O
C	O	R	R	P	E	C	T	U	I
O	N	N	E	T	S	I	L	M	E
V	E	C	N	I	F	I	T	B	D
O	C	E	S	N	O	T	M	L	A
A	K	E	S	E	N	S	E	E	T
E	N	I	L	P	I	C	S	I	D
O	Y	O	U	Y	K	R	A	P	S
N	O	I	T	C	E	R	R	O	C

— — — — — — — —
— — — — — — — — — — ,
— — — — — — — —
— — — — — — —
— — — — — — — — — —
— — — — — .

Accept
Correction
Discipline
Listen
Sparky
Humble

CHAPTER 16:

TRUSTING LOGS?

Go Read Proverbs 16

Good job, troops! We are half way there! Again, make sure that you are still reading the Bible. The nice thing about Proverbs is that the chapters are fairly short. So take the time to actually read them. It won't take that long.

We're going to look at trusting God today. This is very important to look at because it will determine how we live. Before we look at this, check out verse 7, just because it's such a cool verse:

> When people live so that they
> please the LORD, even their enemies
> will make peace with them.
> Proverbs 16:7 NCV

Study Up!

If you study the history of the world you will find that all wars could have been prevented if both sides had done what Jesus wanted. How could this apply to your life?_____

_____

_____

_____

_____

Do you ever feel like there are people that are just plain **hard** to get along with? Those people could be considered your enemies (please don't go and declare war on them). According to this verse, what happens to your

enemies when you live so that you are pleasing to the Lord? They will make peace with you. Why? Because when you live so that you are pleasing to the Lord, you'll be a hard person to hate. **cool**, huh?

Take a Closer Look at: Trusting God

Let's start by looking at what we can learn from this verse.

> *We can make our own plans, but the LORD gives the right answer. Proverbs 16:1 NLT*

Let's take a look at that verse. What does it mean that "the Lord gives the right answer"? Well, what it is saying is that humans can make their plans and be set on them. They think, "This is **exactly** what is going to happen today." But do any of us know what is really going to happen? The Lord is the One who sets our paths. He knows everything. That is one of the really cool things about God. Look at this verse:

> *You have searched me, LORD,*
> *and You know me.*
> *You know when I sit and when I rise;*
> *You perceive my thoughts from afar.*
> *Psalm 139:1-3 NIV*

Wow! God knows even our thoughts! Jesus tells us in Matthew that God knows the number of hairs on our heads! God knows everything. So even if you have this awesome plan, God will still decide what's going to happen. But He loves you and is going to do the very best for you even though to you it might not seem like it is the best.

Quiz 42

1. Enemies can be a strong word, so we think that all of the "enemy passages" aren't for us. But enemies are really just anyone that you don't get along with (and no, you may not train an army to take them out). Who are some of your enemies?

2. What is one way mentioned in this chapter to make peace with your enemies?

3. If we make plans, do they always work out? Why or why not?

4. What is one thing you learned from this section?

5. How are you going to apply what you learned today to your life?

Riddle Me This...

Puzzle #1– SANITY CYPER

Decode using the symbol guide.

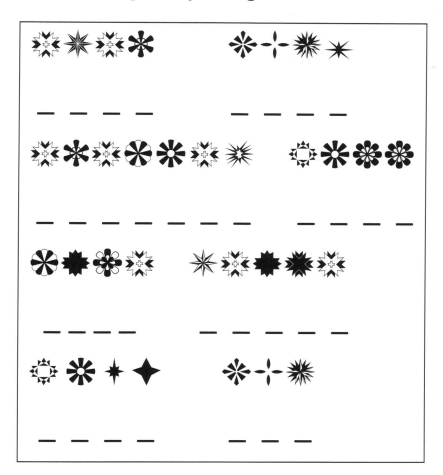

A	✹
C	✸
E	✺
H	◆
I	✳
K	❀
L	✤
M	✿
N	❈
O	⟡
P	✴
R	✶
S	✺
T	✦
U	✷
V	✸
W	⊛
Y	✾

145

Go Read Proverbs 16 Again

Check out this powerful verse:

> Commit your actions to the LORD, and your plans will succeed. Proverbs 16:3 NLT

What does it mean to commit your plans to the Lord? It kind of sounds WEIRD, doesn't it? Well, let's take a look at it. When you commit something to someone, it's like you hand it over to them. When two people get married, they hand over their wants and desires to the other person. When you commit your life to God, you hand over your life into His hands. How do we hand over our life to God? Well, we give Him our choices. We make choices that bring Him honor and glory. So when you commit your actions to the Lord, you hand them over to Him. When you commit something to God, He might change it.

Real Life

Today when you come across a situation when you want to do it your way, let God have control and it will go a lot better for you in the long run.

When you commit your actions to God, you're letting Him have control of your life. Does letting God have complete control of your life sound like fun? No, not really. I mean, it's fun to have control of your own life. But do you remember the first verse that we looked at? That verse says that even your enemies will make peace with you when you follow God. And the verse that we just looked at said that all of your plans will succeed when you follow God. Also, remember that when you follow God, you are making wise decisions. So there are tons of blessings that come with following God because there are tons of blessings that come with being wise.

Let's take a look at a couple more verses:

> *We can make our plans, but the LORD determines our steps.*
> *Proverbs 16:9 NLT*
> *There is a path before each person that seems right, but it ends in death.*
> *Proverbs 16:25 NLT*

Even though these verses are very close to the ones that we've looked at, we can still learn from them. Proverbs 16:9 is telling us that even though we make plans, God will still have His way in our lives. We can plan all we want, but the Lord's plan will still win over ours. Proverbs 16:25 tells us that we do not know what is best. Sometimes, we can be so sure that we're right and somebody else seems so wrong. However, we are often deceived by our own sin. Jesus called it a log in our eyes. He said that often we see each other's sins a lot sooner and clearer than we see our own (you can read about this in Matthew 7:3-5). We can even think that we are right when we are actually very wrong. We can say, "Oh, buying this new Ultrasonic Transformer Laser Bike is the best thing I can do." But because of our sin, we often can't see that we are totally wrong. That is why it is so good to trust in God. God knows what is right, and often, we ourselves don't know what is right.

Quiz 43

1. Define "commit".

2. What does Proverbs promise us will happen if we commit what we do to the Lord?

3. What did Jesus mean when He talked about having logs in your eyes?

4. What is one thing you learned from this section?

5. How are you going to apply what you learned today to your life?

Verse of Fame

Proverbs 16:18

Pride goes before destruction, a haughty spirit before a fall.

Puzzle #2- Code Crusher

Decoding directions contained in the letter... (just read the letter below)

highway the about talks verse This take always people righteous That destruction avoids path that how And stake at lives their putting than Rather

- Proverbs 16:11
- Proverbs 16:17
- Proverbs 16:18
- Proverbs 16:30

___ ___ ___ ___ ___ ___

___ ___ ___ ___ ___

___ ___ ___ ___ ___ ___

___ ___ ___ ___ ___ ___

SuperSpiesRUs.INC
321 SuperSneak Ln.
Hidden, Hiding 54321
1-800-ISPYONU

Top Secret
This Letter Permitted to
Authorized Personnel Only

Dear CodeCrusher:

We had our dear spy-employee Mixup Dave take a picture of a code that CodeMaker was writing on an alley wall. Although, Dave *can* get a bit mixed up about taking pictures. (Remember the mirror codecrusher? Yeah... that's Dave.) Unscramble the poetic puzzler and circle the reference of the mystery verse.

Good Luck,
Mr. SuperSneaky

CHAPTER 17:

Crooks in Squirrel Pajamas

Go Read Proverbs 17:1-18

Let's focus on your relationship with your **parents** this time. Do you ever feel like it's hard to obey your **parents**? Do you feel like they're kind of old, listen to some weird type of stone-age music, and aren't as good at video games as you are? Well, God placed them over you. He wants you to obey your parents because when you do, it brings Him honor and glory. Even though most of our parents aren't really that weird, we still need to honor them. If you have trouble with this, then you need to ask God to help you change. We all need to see change in our lives! It is very, very important to make an effort to apply the stuff that we learn in the Bible. Look at this verse:

BAD

IDEA

If you have a proud heart, you won't learn anything from Proverbs. Have a heart that wants to change and a mind that's ready to rewind and rethink.

> Do what God's teaching says;
> when you only listen and do nothing,
> you are fooling yourselves. James 1:22 NCV

If you are reading Proverbs and saying, "Yeah, yeah. I already know all this. Ho-hum," and you do nothing to change yourself; you are acting like a fool. So listen carefully, and actually use it in your life. And guess what. That's **another** way of being wise.

Go Read Proverbs 17:19-20

Alrighty gang, check out this verse:

> *Whoever loves a quarrel loves sin; whoever builds a high gate invites destruction. Proverbs 17:19 NIV*

Let's take a look at the second part. Ok, let's pretend that you're a crook. You want to break into a house and steal a lot of money (this is another one of those things that I don't want to hear that you tried). So you pick a neighborhood and decide that you're going to **ROB** one of the houses. You go to look and see which house you want to **ROB**. You're a bit disappointed to find that all of the houses look exactly the same. But wait! There at the end of the street! You see a very *fancy* and expen$ive-looking house! That's the one! Why did you pick that one? Well, because it looks a lot better than all of the other ones. All the other houses are plain and **boring**, but this one looks really, really NICE. Many rich people like to show off their wealth, and sometimes they do that by living in huge houses with

cool, **BIG** gates. You can tell that those people are rich and have lots of nice things. It's like they're inviting you to rob them. Later that night, you rob those people blind, and take off to Hawaii... until you get caught.

Why did I give you this weird example? Have you ever met a kid who brags a lot about how much money he or his parents have? He's making himself like that gigantic house at the end of that block. He's inviting destruction,

151

just like the house practically invited you to rob it. So don't brag about anything, because its like sticking a sign on your back that says, "Hurt me!" It's also like putting a **BIG**, *fancy*, golden gate in front of your house. You're just asking for destruction to come and get you.

Quiz 44

1. At the very beginning of this section we talked about **parents**. Why should we show them respect?

2. What does bragging invite?

3. What does the Bible mean when it talks about building a high gate?

4. What is one thing you learned from this section?

5. How are you going to apply what you learned today to your life?

Riddle Me This...

Puzzle #1 – CROSSWORD CRAM

Parents

Relationship

Wise

Apply

Change

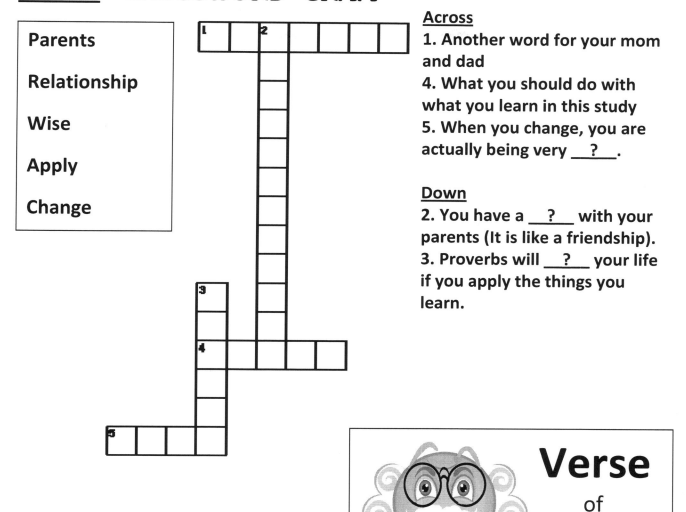

Across

1. Another word for your mom and dad
4. What you should do with what you learn in this study
5. When you change, you are actually being very ___?___.

Down

2. You have a ___?___ with your parents (It is like a friendship).
3. Proverbs will ___?___ your life if you apply the things you learn.

Verse of Fame

Proverbs 17:17

A friend loves at all times, and a brother is born for a time of adversity.

Go Read Proverbs 17:19-20 Again

Ok, go back and read verse 19 again. Do you ever feel like you love quarrels? If you said, "Yeah, they are so cute!" I wasn't talking about the little animals with the bushy tails. To quarrel is to squabble (not like a turkey!). It's like arguing. Do you ever like to argue? I sometimes think that it is loads of fun. There's something about it that is just exciting. Especially with my siblings. However, what's that verse say about people who love to quarrel? It says that they love sin. So you can't be righteous *and* love to quarrel. Remember that the next time that you feel like you just *have* to fight with someone.

Go Read Proverbs 17:21-28 *and*

Take a Closer Look at: Being a Good Kid

Here is some more of that reputation stuff again. Read these next verses carefully and try to understand what they mean:

> It is painful to be the parent of a fool; there is no joy for the father of a rebel. Proverbs 17:21 NLT
>
> Foolish children bring grief to their father and bitterness to the one who gave them birth. Proverbs 17:25 NLT

Remember how I said that your actions reflect on your parents? Well, they do, very much so. When you do something foolish, it damages people's view of your parents. This can be kind of hard, because it is hard to fix a broken reputation. It can be extremely painful when your friends never see you the same as they did before you ruined your reputation. Another reason that it can really be painful to be the parent of the fool is because they love you so much. How does that make it painful? Well, your parents love you *way* more than you can ever imagine. It's like they feel your pain. That's how much they love you. When you do something wrong, your parents know the consequences of your actions, and they kind of feel your pain before you do. Isn't that crazy? That's how much they love you! Let me ask you a question: when you do what is right, do you think that your parents are thrilled? You'd better bet your Barbie Tonka truck pajamas they are! They love it when you do what is right, and so does God. So live in a way that is pleasing to God and your parents.

Real Life

Tell your parents how much you appreciate them today, and ask them if there's anything you can do for them.

Quiz 45

1. What does "quarrel" mean?

2. Fill in the blank, "Whoever loves to quarrel loves _____."

3. Is it possible to be righteous and love to quarrel? Why or why not?

4. What is one thing you learned from this section?

5. How are you going to apply what you learned today to your life?

Puzzle #2- Code Crusher

Decoding directions contained in the letter... (just read the letter below)

SuperSpiesRUs.INC
321 SuperSneak Ln.
Hidden, Hiding 54321
1-800-ISPYONU

Top Secret
This Letter Permitted to
Authorized Personnel Only

CONFIDENTIAL

Dear CodeCrusher:

We were investigating today's reading in your book (this one, actually) looking for clues that might lead us to the identity of Thomas Michaels. It wasn't very helpful. But we did find these odd dots everywhere in the last section of text (see photo below). We also found this slip of paper in the book. It must have slipped in. I think it has something to do with the dots, but I don't really know.

Good Luck,

Mr. SuperSneaky

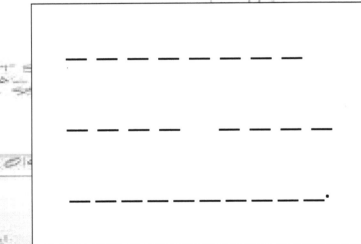

Remember that whenever you read Proverbs, it is helpful to think of a picture in your head. The first verses of chapter 8 talk about where wisdom is **standing**. Now, is wisdom a real life person, whose voice we can really hear? We all know that she isn't. So why does Proverbs tell us where she is standing? This is a trick that some writers use called personification, which takes something that's not alive and compares it to a person or some other living object. So, an being (which we already knew). You might be

— — — — — — —

— — — — — — —

— — — — — — — — — .

CHAPTER 18:

SHHHHHHHHHHHHHHHHHHHH! LisTEN.

Go Read Proverbs 18:1-7

Have you ever gone out walking in the woods, or maybe in the mountains? Did you ever stop to just listen? It's incredible what you can hear when you listen.

Real Life

When you come to a quiet moment during the day, take a minute and thank God for giving you this beautiful world.

You're away from all of the cars, the noises, the people, the French fries. (It's ok. You'll go back.) You can hear all kinds of things like elephants, tigers, and bears. Just kidding. You *can* hear streams, birds, insects, and the wind in the leaves. You feel like you could hear an ant sneeze. It's beautiful! We don't get to do that very often; especially in our country and the world we are growing up in. Everybody is in their **Fast**-moving cars, talking on their **Fast**-moving cell phones, and listening to their **Fast**-moving music on their iPods®. We don't get a chance to just stop and listen to anything very much. But it is good to SLOW DOWN and listen. God wants us to do that with our friends and families too.

Take a Closer Look at: Wickedness

Take a look at this verse:

> *Fools have no interest in understanding; they only want to air their own opinions. Proverbs 18:2 NLT*

Do you know what it's called when a news announcer or a D.J. is on the radio live? It's called being on the air. So take a quick look at that verse again. Fools want to air their own opinions. Sometimes when you get into an argument with someone, they don't really listen to anything that you say. Instead they keep giving you arguments that don't really make any sense with what you're talking about. I *HATE* to tell you this, but according to that verse, they don't care about anything you say. They just want to show off their "smarts." That's why they're fools. They don't ever listen to anything, including Wisdom. Are you ever like that? Do you ever want to just "air" your thoughts? I know it's easy to do that, but really be careful to listen to other people's corrections or thoughts. Just remember this verse next time you're being an airhead.

Quiz 46

1. What simple command do we tell you to do at the *very* start of the chapter? Why is this important?

2. It is fine to have your own opinion, but sometimes it can get dangerous. According to Proverbs 18:2, when does listening to your own opinions become dangerous?

3. Who do the foolish listen to?

4. What is one thing you learned from this section?

5. How are you going to apply what you learned today to your life?

Riddle Me This...

Puzzle #1 – **Block Brain!**

Unscramble the tiles to reveal a hidden message. This is the first tile. If You need help, go ask your parents to get you started.

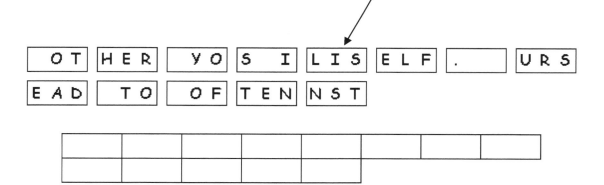

| O T | H E R | | Y O | S | I | L I S | E L F | . | | U R S |
| E A D | | T O | | O F | T E N | N S T | | | | |

Go Read Proverbs 18:1-7 Again

A big part of listening is what you're listening to. You shouldn't be a good listener if you're listening to something bad. Check out these verses:

> *Wise words are like deep waters; wisdom flows from the wise like a bubbling brook. Proverbs 18:4 NLT*
>
> *Fools' words get them into constant quarrels; they are asking for a beating. Proverbs 18:6 NLT*
>
> *The mouths of fools are their ruin; they trap themselves with their lips. Proverbs 18:7 NLT*

Wow, those sure are some **CRAZY** verses! Let's look at verse 4. Do you remember how I said that when you go into the woods it's fun to listen to the different sounds? Well, have you ever heard a bubbling brook? It's very different from a river. The river sounds like it's moving too fast; it kind of sounds like a roar. But a bubbling brook sounds very different. It sounds like it's just... fun. That's how the wise words should sound to our ears. We should kind of get excited about listening to them, because we know exactly what comes with wisdom.

Who Knew?

Sometimes listening to wisdom can be fun, but sometimes it can be really hard. It goes both ways, but God wants us to, "count it all joy," or be cheerful through it all.

Ok, if listening to the wise is like listening to a bubbling brook, what is it like to listen to the fool? Well, let's look at what their words do for them. Do you remember Billy Peanut-Plane from Chapter 14? Do you remember how his bragging caused his friends to turn against him? This is sort of like that. A fool's words get them into constant quarrels. We already know what loving an argument is like. This verse is telling us that the foolish person always says something **silly** that gets him into trouble. Let's look at the third verse. What does it say that the fool's mouth is to them? It says that it is their ruin, right? This agrees with the second verse, which says that the fool's tongue is like a rod that beats them. Isn't that crazy? Your own tongue beating you like a rod! Wow. Our speech is pretty powerful. I know what I want my speech to be! And I know what I would rather listen to!

Quiz 47

1. How should you feel about listening to wisdom?

2. What is the result of a fool's words? (Proverbs 18:6)

3. A fool's words lead to an argument. Loving an argument is the same as loving sin. Loving sin leads to death. Using that information, why do you think fool's words are bad?

4. What is one thing you learned from this section?

5. How are you going to apply what you learned today to your life?

Riddle Me This...

Puzzle #2 – CROSSWORD CRAM

Quarrels

Fool's

Shouldn't

Excited

Bubbling Brook

Mouths

P.S. – Don't put in any spaces or apostrophes (').

Across
2. A fool's words get him into constant _____.
5. The _____'_ tongue is like a rod that beats him.
6. The _____ of fools are their ruin (Proverbs 18:7 NIV)

Down
1. Wisdom flows from the wise like a _____ _____.
3. We should get _____ about listening to wisdom.
4. You _____'__ be a good listener if you're listening to something bad.

Verse of Fame

Proverbs 18:18
Casting the lot settles disputes and keeps strong opponents apart.

Go Read Proverbs 18:8-12

> *Rumors are dainty morsels that sink deep into one's heart.*
> *Proverbs 18:8 NLT*

Do you know what gossip is? It might sound something like this:

Little naughty girl 1: Did you, like, hear what that new girl, like, eats for breakfast?!

Little naughty girl 2: No. Like, what?!

Little naughty girl 1: She eats, like, peas and celery mixed with rhubarb!

Little naughty girl 2: Like, wow! That's, like, disgusting! Like, where'd you hear this?

Little naughty girl 1: Like, that girl Suzie Cuzie, the one with the, like, gigantic lips. She heard it from like her cousin Fred, like, the one with the big hair.

Little naughty girl 2: Like, that new girl's a loser! I'm gonna go, like, put on enough makeup so that, like, I can't open my eyes.

Yup, that's how gossip goes. The truth is that the new girl actually likes to eat Cocoa Puffs™. That's how rumors and gossip start. A rumor starts when someone says something that doesn't need to be said or that is not necessarily true about someone else. What does that verse say about rumors? It says that they're like dainty morsels. Dainty means *fancy*. Have you ever had Doritos™? It's like you can't get enough of them; you just want to keep eating and eating them. I love Doritos™… anyway, a rumor is like a Doritos™ chip. You just can't get enough of rumors or gossip just like you can always eat more Doritos™. But gossip sticks to your heart and mind (just like the Doritos™ dust sticks to your fingers). Once you hear a rumor about someone, you will NEVER see them the same. So be careful with what you listen to.

Go Read Proverbs 18:13-24

Ok, get a load of these two verses:

> To answer before listening—
> that is folly and shame. Proverbs 18:13 NIV
>
> The first to speak in court sounds right—
> until the cross-examination begins. Proverbs 18:17 NLT

Does your mom ever say something like this, "Alberta, go pick up…" and you yell, "NO MOM, CAN'T YOU SEE THAT I'M BUSY?" (You would never do that!) And she says to you, "Alberta, I was going to tell you to go pick up the million dollars that I won from across the street." You would feel pretty foolish, wouldn't you? Well, you should, because that's what spouting off before listening to the facts is. **Bad Alberta**.

Ok, let's say you're having lunch with Sammy Billy Jones. Little Sammy decides that the hamburger that he is eating would look a lot better smeared on the wall than it would sitting nicely on his plate. So he throws his burger like a world class baseball pitcher right onto your mom's favorite part of the wall. Your mom walks in, and… (Yeah, kids, you know what's coming!) asks, "**WHO THREW A HAMBURGER AT MY FAVORITE PART OF THE WALL?**"

Sammy jumps out of his chair, points his ketchup-covered finger at *you*, and shouts, "**I DID IT!** No wait… **HE DID IT!**" Your mom turns toward you and says, "Bobby…?" You calmly explain to your mother that it's impossible for you to have thrown a hamburger because your hamburger is still sitting on your plate, and besides, you broke your arm last week throwing meatloaf at your *dad*'s favorite part of the wall. Finally, your mom sees that it was *Sammy* and sends him back to his house.

The first person always sounds right until the second person tells his side of the story. Your mom was convinced that it was you who threw the hamburger based on Sammy's story. But when you told her what happened she got the whole picture. That's what happens in court a lot. Someone will say, "He threw the hamburger." But the story really doesn't come out until the jury hears both sides. What was the moral of the story? Never throw your hamburger at your mom's favorite part of the wall, and always, always listen to both sides of a story.

Quiz 48

1. How is gossip like lying (think back to the little naughty girl story)?

2. Spouting off is kind of like interrupting. Thinking back to the million dollars across the street example, why is it foolish to spout off?

3. Who does it hurt when you don't listen to both sides of the story? Does it hurt only you or does it hurt other people too?

4. What is one thing you learned from this section?

5. How are you going to apply what you learned today to your life?

Puzzle #3– *Code Crusher*

Decoding directions contained in the letter... (just read the letter below)

Rum orsar eno tgoo
dtolis tento .Whe nyo
ulis tento the m,yo
unev erloo kat peo
plet hesam eaga in.j
ustb eca refult owat
chwh atyo ulis ten
toan dsa y.

SuperSpiesRUs.INC
321 SuperSneak Ln.
Hidden, Hiding 54321
1-800-ISPYONU

Top Secret
This Letter Permitted to
Authorized Personnel Only

Dear CodeCrusher:

We were e-mailed this weird piece of
paper. We sent you a projector. I hope that
you can set it up and project it on your
desk. Look at the words – I think it's similar
to a jumbled phrase. Just see if you can
make out the words. Then, write the
phrase on the piece of paper provided.

Good Luck,
Mr. SuperSneaky

CHAPTER 19:

Of Smashed Thumbs and Liars

Go Read Proverbs 19

Let's talk about lies. This is another thing that is really, really important to God, because God *is* TRUTH. Telling the TRUTH is so important that it made God's top ten list: the Ten Commandments. Right now, stay tuned, because we'll be right back after this short break.

Hey kids, have you ever seen Proverbs 19:11? It's a pretty cool verse. Let's take a closer look at it.

> *A person's wisdom yields patience;*
> *it is to one's glory to overlook an offense.*
> *Proverbs 19:11 NIV*

What is this verse saying? A person's wisdom yields patience? Do you know what *yields* means? Ok, today, pretend that you are a **farmer**. You want to plant some corn. So you *buy seed that will give you a good crop.* Ok, another way to say what I just said is *you buy seed that will "yield" a good crop.* Yield means to give. You might have heard some people say, "You need to yield your life to Christ." It means to *give* your life to Christ. You might have seen a sign on the street that says "YIELD!" It means to let other cars go first; you're *giving* them their turn. So what does it mean when it says that wisdom yields **patience**? It means that wisdom *gives* you patience. Do you ever feel like you have absolutely no patience at all? Well, by getting wisdom, you are getting patience. What does the last part of the verse say? It is to one's glory to overlook an offense. When you overlook something, you miss it. So, let's say you accidentally spill your Legos all over the floor, and you go to pick up every single piece. When you accidentally missed a piece, you overlooked it. Don't worry. When your dad steps on it, you'll know where to find it.

Study Up!

Write out a time in the Bible when someone forgave someone else (or overlooked an offense).

_____

_____

_____

Quiz 49

1. We sometimes lie. The cool thing about God is that He is full of __?__ . (Hint: Look at the very start of this chapter.)

2. What does yield mean?

3. Now, using your definition of yield, what does the Bible mean when it says, "Wisdom yields patience"?

4. What is one thing you learned from this section?

5. How are you going to apply what you learned today to your life?

Riddle Me This...

<u>**Puzzle #1**</u> – NUMBER CODE

Fill in the blanks with the letters that match the numbers.

❶   ⑯❺⑱⑲⑮⑭'⑲   ■❾⑲❹⑮⑬   ♦❾❺⑫❹⑲

⑯❶⑳❾❺⑭❸❺

___

___ ___ ___ ___ ___ ___ , ___

___ ___ ___ ___ ___ ___

___ ___ ___ ___ ___

___ ___ ___ ___ ___ ___ ___ ___

A	❶
C	❸
D	❹
E	❺
I	❾
L	⑫
M	⑬
N	⑭
O	⑮
P	⑯
R	⑱
S	⑲
T	⑳
W	■
Y	♦

Go Read Proverbs 19 Again

Go back and read Proverbs 19:11 again so that you remember it. Have you ever heard the expression, "Oh, that sticks out like a sore THUMB"? What's that mean? Well, your THUMB is your most important finger. In fact, it's so

important, that it's not even considered a finger. You're probably looking at your THUMB saying, "Wow! I've never noticed that before." Well, if you never ever want to say that sentence again, grab a hammer and smash your THUMB as hard as you can. You will never say that again. You use your THUMB all of the

time, and when it's sore, you always remember that it's sore. That's where that saying comes from. Ok, why did I tell you this? The Bible tells us to overlook an offense. When someone hurts you, the Bible wants you to overlook it like you overlooked that Lego piece! Whenever someone hurts you, it can feel like it is a sore THUMB to you. It is really, really hard to overlook a sore

Real Life

When someone hurts you today, overlook the offense, just like that Lego piece. Forgive the person who hurt you.

THUMB, because you are constantly reminded of it. Just like you have to try really hard to overlook a sore THUMB, you have to try really hard to overlook an offense. But you can do it, and when you do, it will be to your glory. That means that you will be honored because you made the choice to overlook an offense. Cool, huh? So the next time your little brother flushes your action figures down the toilet, remember that verse.

Quiz 50

1. What would "taking an offense as a sore **THUMB**" mean?

2. What would "taking an offense as a **Lego** piece" mean?

3. Does God want us humans to see an offense as a sore **THUMB** or as a **Lego** piece?

4. What is one thing you learned from this section?

5. How are you going to apply what you learned today to your life?

Riddle Me This...

Puzzle #2 – CaPiTaL CrAzY

Take all of the capital letters (yes, ALL of them) and write them in the blanks below, and you will come up with a wise phrase.

fOrgiVing pEople is so haRd! it is not Like anything else we ever have tO dO. It's one of the hardest things that in our Knowledge that we have to do. but we All kNow that we need tO Forgive others, just as he ForgavE us, Not becauSe he was forced to, but out of lovE, for our sins.

— — — — — — — —   — —   — — — — — — —

Go Read Proverbs 19 (yes, *again*)

And we're back! Let's take a look at these verses:

> *A witness who lies will not go free; liars will never escape.*
> *Proverbs 19:5 NCV*

Have you ever told a lie? If you said no, now you might as well say yes, because you just lied. Everybody lies, except God. Let me ask you a question: what is the penalty for lying? Well, the punishment for any sin is death. Let's take a look at this short verse: *Romans 6:23* (look at the scroll off to the side). A wage is what you earn for the things that you do. So what we get for the sins that we do is death. The type of death that it is talking about here is the opposite of eternal life. It is eternal death, which is being separated from God forever in hell. So what we get for our sins is hell. Even the "little" sins are serious enough that they must be paid for. But don't worry. Jesus has already paid the penalty. Look at the second verse. Liars never escape punishment - nobody ever escapes punishment. We only escape punishment because Jesus took our punishment for us on the cross. Check out this verse:

True False

☐ ☑

> *For the wages of sin is death, but the free gift of God is eternal life through Christ Jesus our Lord. NIV*

> *It is better to be poor and honest than to be foolish and tell lies. Proverbs 19:1 NCV*

Is it really better to be poor and honest than to be a liar? Well, remember that liars can never escape punishment. When we lie, and we don't believe in Jesus, we have to pay for our own sins. Nobody wants to be poor, but being a liar is worse than being poor; because it's easier to live poor than have to pay for our own sins. Crazy, huh?

Let's take a look at one more verse:

> *People want others to be loyal, so it is better to be poor than to be a liar. Proverbs 19:22 NCV*

Did you know that people are desperate to be loved? Everybody needs to be loved. God made us so that we could receive His love and other people's love. Now, what do you think happens when we lie to our friends all of the time? Most likely they won't really want to hang around us anymore, because they can't trust us. This verse says that being a liar is worse than being poor. God wants us to be honest in our relationships. Why? Because that will reflect well on Him. So live an honest life. It will benefit you in every way.

Quiz 51

1. What is a wage?

2. Lying leads to death. Can you remember some other things in Proverbs that lead to death?

Verse
of
Fame

Proverbs 19:21

Many are the plans in a person's heart, but it is the LORD's purpose that prevails.

3. In the last two sentences of the text, we gave you another reason to avoid lying. What is the other reason?

4. What is one thing you learned from this section?

5. How are you going to apply what you learned today to your life?

Puzzle #3 – CodeCrusher

Decoding directions contained in letter... (just read the letter)

SuperSpiesRUs.INC
321 SuperSneak Ln.
Hidden, Hiding 54321
1-800-ISPYONU

Top Secret
This Letter Permitted to
Authorized Personneal Only

Dear CodeCrusher:

Yep, today's package has lots of papers. We even went into the next page! Look at the sheet of paper below. As you read down the list, if it's a lie, write out the first letter of the lie in the lie column <u>on the next page</u> (Example 6. H). If it's truth, write the first letter in the truth column <u>on the next page</u> (Example 8. T). When they are all filled in, you should notice that the numbering is way messed up. So what you're going to do, like the example, is take the letter to the right of the number on the truth/lie paper. Then, write it in above its matching number on the paper below the truth/lie one. Hope you can get it!

Good Luck,
Mr. SuperSneaky

Having the most toys makes you the best

Lots of people have never lied

DO THIS ONE NEXT

The Bible never lies

Lying leads to life

Everyone wears blue T-shirts on Friday

Time lost can't ever come back gain

Every person needs to believe in Jesus to get into heaven

Resting *can* be good

The boogie monster lives under your bed

Having God is a good thing

Telling the truth is never the right thing to do

Underneath your clothes is your skin

Lies	Truth
6. H	8.
2.	7.
3.	12.
4.	10.
11.	1.
5.	9.

__ __ __ __   __ H __   __ __ __ __ __
1 2 3 4   5 6 7   8 9 10 11 12

CHAPTER 20:

LIPS OF GOLD? OR BETTER?

Go Read Proverbs 20

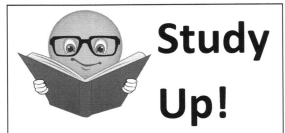

Study Up!

Name one time since you started this study that you were about to do something wrong, but you decided not to because you knew it would reflect poorly on God.

_____

_____

We need to take another look at our speech. Why? Because when God talks to us, we'd better listen. But when God *repeats* something, you should put on your ultra-hearing helmet so that you don't miss what He has to say to you. God addresses our speech a lot, so it's important that we watch what we say. Why? Because what we say reflects back on Him (that is one of the topics we studied in Chapter 12).

Let's jump right into this passage.

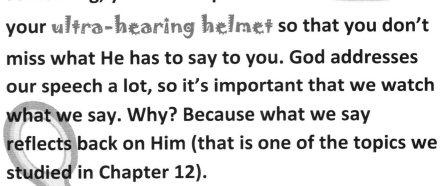

Many people claim to be loyal, but it is hard to find a trustworthy person. Proverbs 20:6 NCV

What is this verse saying? Well, people who claim to be loyal are not always loyal. If you have been reading Proverbs you have probably noticed a few verses that are about **friendships**, like these:

A man of too many friends comes to ruin, but there is a friend who sticks closer than a brother. Proverbs 18:24 NASB

With their words, the godless destroy their friends, but knowledge will rescue the righteous. Proverbs 11:9 NLT

Ok, let me ask you a hard question. No cheating! From these three verses, does it seem like all **friends** are truly your **friends**? _____.

Just like all people who say that they are your **friends** aren't truly your **friends**, not all people who claim to be loyal are really loyal. Do you ever make claims about yourself that are not true? It might be just a white lie. We have got to make sure that only truth comes from our mouths. Even if a lie doesn't seem like it's a big deal to us, it's a **BIG** deal to God. Be honest with your **friends**. So what does that verse say about someone who is trustworthy? They are really hard to find, right? Do you want to be a person who is known for being trustworthy? Believe it or not, you can make choices to become that person. If you keep your word, work hard, and are a good friend, God will richly bless your life.

Quiz 52

1. We keep on talking about how to live a good life. Why do we need to live good lives? Look back in Chapter 12 (page 107) at the reflection picture if you need to.

2. According to Proverbs 20:6, what is one quality of a trustworthy friend?

3. What are some things you can do to become a trustworthy friend? (You just read this! Look at the end of this section.)

4. What is one thing you learned from this section?

5. How are you going to apply what you learned today to your life?

Riddle Me This...

Puzzle #1 – *MAZE MAYHEM*

Carol and John are new to their school, and want good friends. Can you help them find Craig and Melissa, the most trustworthy kids in the school?

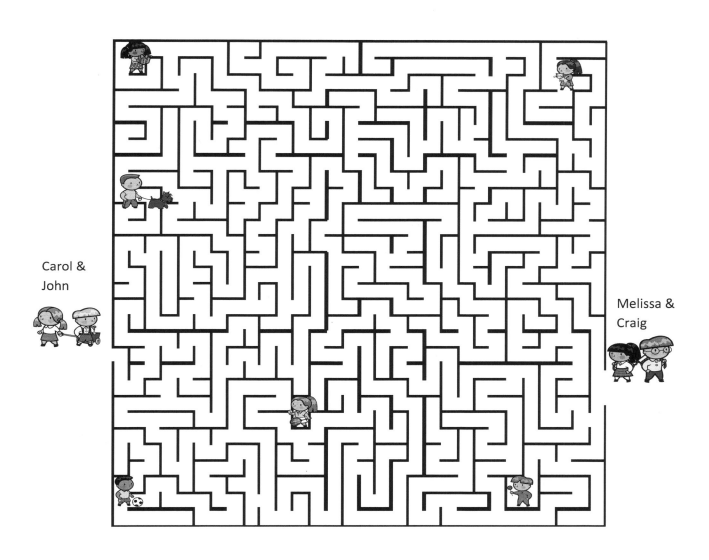

Go Read Proverbs 20 Again

Ok, this next verse is so cool. Check this verse out!

> *Even children are known by their behavior; their actions show*
> *if they are innocent and good. Proverbs 20:11 NCV*

Isn't that cool to think about? You are known by your behavior! Ok, let's go back to that time that you were the **crook** in Chapter 17. Let's say that you got caught by the police. They took you to the jail. There they took your picture, fingerprinted you, wrote down your name, your address, and all of your information. They say that from now on you will be called **Crook Kelly**. Why? Because they know that your actions made you a **crook**. Now, what if instead of being a **crook**, you made little CANDY canes and gave them to homeless children. Then you would be called CANDY KELLY. Which one would you rather be known as? **Crook Kelly** or CANDY KELLY? Your actions and words define your reputation. Even though you are just a kid, you can already make yourself stand out. I bet you thought that you had to wait until you're older! Nope. You can already set the course for your life and make wise decisions. How cool is that? It can also be kind of scary, because if you make bad decisions, you will be traveling down a very dangerous path. Your decisions now will affect your decisions in the future. So make wise choices or you will ruin your life.

Quiz 53

1. What we do affects our reputation. Like, if you passed out CANDY, you would be called CANDY Kelly, and if you stole stuff, you would be called crook Kelly. So what should we do to keep a good name?

2. What happens if you don't do what you wrote as an answer on the last question?

3. Who determines our reputation?

4. What is one thing you learned from this section?

5. How are you going to apply what you learned today to your life?

Riddle Me This...

Puzzle #2 – RE + 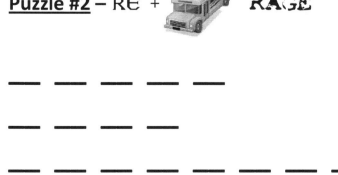 RAGE

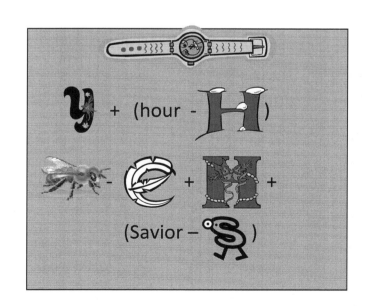

— — — — —

— — — —

— — — — — — — — —

Go Read Proverbs 20 (yes, *again*)

The next verse is also very amazing. Did you know that you can make your lips a rare jewel? All that you need to do is drink a whole bunch of sugar-water while plugging your NOSE. Ok, I'm just kidding about the whole sugar-water thing; and you can't really make your lips a rare jewel. You can only make your lips *like* a rare jewel: a very rare jewel. How? Well, read this verse to find out:

> Gold there is, and rubies in abundance, but lips that speak knowledge are a rare jewel. Proverbs 20:15 NIV

"Wait! There isn't an abundance of rubies!" you might say. "I don't even know what abundance means…" Well, to answer your question, an abundance of something means that there are a lot of them. Why does the Bible say that there are a lot of rubies? Well, first of all, there *are* a lot of rubies, but they are still very difficult to find. Second, if you took a look at all of the rubies in the world and all of the people who speak knowledge, there would be far more RUBIES than wise people! WOW! Wise people don't seem like they should be that hard to find! But they are. Think about it this way. Let's say that you are with ten of your friends. Chances are that one of them has some type of ruby in his house like maybe on a necklace or a ring. Maybe even a couple of your friends have rubies in their houses. Now think about this: how many of these ten friends speak knowledge? Probably none of them do. I bet you guys talk about your new XBOX™, IPOD™, **hairspray**, or your co·m.pu·ter more than you talk about the stuff that you learned in Sunday school. I know that is how I can be with my friends. Do you realize how that verse can be so true? Do you want to change? You could be like a very rare jewel. All you have to do is talk about stuff that really matters. You might be saying, "But it's so hard!" I know it is. I remember that one time I had a friend that was going through a hard time. The situation kind of became an emergency. I couldn't just let myself talk carelessly with him anymore; we had to switch our talking to more serious stuff. We still talk casually, but we now talk a lot about more important stuff. Here's one idea how you can begin more serious conversations. You can write a verse down on a piece of paper and just pick one friend to give it to. That can be an easy way to start. Don't let your friends get into "emergency" situations, without being right there for them with your words. I know it's hard. But that's what God has for our lives. He wants our words to actually mean something. The Bible tells us that our words can either build up or destroy others. God wants us to be builder-uppers with our words!

Real Life

Do it! Write down a verse on a sheet of paper and give it to a friend. Don't have a verse to give? Try this one.

Be on your guard; stand firm in the faith; be courageous; be strong. Do everything in love.
1 Corinthians 16:13-14

Quiz 54

1. What does abundance mean?

2. What do you have to do if you want to be a "ruby lip" among your friends?

3. Is it easy or hard to find "ruby lips"?

4. What is one thing you learned from this section?

5. How are you going to apply what you learned today to your life?

Verse of Fame

Proverbs 20:1

Wine is a mocker and beer a brawler; whoever is led astray by them is not wise.

Puzzle #3- Code Crusher

Decoding directions contained in the letter... (just read the letter below)

SuperSpiesRUs.INC
321 SuperSneak Ln.
Hidden, Hiding 54321
1-800-ISPYONU

Top Secret
This Letter Permitted to
Authorized Personnel Only

Dear CodeCrusher:

We got this email with all this weird stuff on it. I think there could be some kind of hidden meaning behind it, but I don't really know how to find it, and all of those circles seem kind of fishy.

    Good Luck,
       Mr. SuperSneaky

Who died on the cross for your sins?

◯ __ __ __ __

You are known by your ___?___

__ ◯ __ __ __ __ __ __

You need to find ___?___ friends.

__ __ __ __ ◯ __ __ __ __ __

Our words can either build up or ___?___ down.

__ ◯ __ __

Many people claim to be ___?___, but it is hard to find a trustworthy person.
Proverbs 20:6

__ __ __ ◯ __

You lips should become like a rare ___ ___ ___ ___ ___

CHAPTER 21:

I KNOW WHERE YOU LIVE!

Go Read Proverbs 21

I hope you still have that ultra-hearing helmet handy, because you're going to need it. We've seen the **wicked man**, THE FOOL, and the **SLUGGARD** over and over in Proverbs. Well, Chapter 21 is no different. We're going to take another look at the wicked man and his sidekicks.

Check out this very interesting verse:

> *People may be right in their own eyes,*
> *but the LORD examines their heart. Proverbs 21:2 NLT*

This verse tells us that person thinks that his ways are right, but the Lord weighs the heart. Sometimes we think that we know what is right, even when we don't. Huh? Ok, let me put it this way. Let's say you go to a birthday party, and you're about to eat some cake. As everybody's waiting for cake, your friend whispers to you, "Ooh, I think it's CHOCOLATE cake! I love CHOCOLATE cake!" You kind of get excited because you like CHOCOLATE cake too. But, when the cake is brought out, you see that it is VANILLA cake. Your friend squeals like a little girl (because she *is* a little girl) and says, "Yeah, CHOCOLATE cake!"

So you decide to tell her the truth, "Um, hello? That isn't chocolate cake."

186

She says, "YES, it is."

And you say, "No, it's not."

"YES, it is."

"No, it's not."

BAD IDEA

Some people think that you can just make up something and believe in it. They say that truth changes. Don't listen to people who tell you that truth can change. God is truth, and He never changes.

Finally the cake is cut and you're like, "Yeah, this is going to teach her." She takes a bite and says, "MMM! I love CHOCOLATE cake!" Surprised, you take a bite yourself only to find that you're eating a piece of VANILLA cake. She's crazy.

Now that little girl believed that the cake was CHOCOLATE. I mean, she really, really believed it. Just because she believed it, does that mean that she was right? No, of course not! Some people believe that whatever you strongly believe in is the truth. Is that right? I mean, that little girl really, really, really, REALLY believed that cake was CHOCOLATE. But even though she strongly believed that the cake was CHOCOLATE, she didn't believe in the truth. The same is true for any religion. People can believe as hard as they want about anything, but if it isn't the truth, it doesn't matter how hard they believe in it. So how can we know that what we believe is the truth? Well, we know that everything that God says is true, because God does not lie (if you think I'm wrong, check out Numbers 23:19). If we want to believe in the truth, all that we have to do is look to God. If we want to look to God, all we have to do is look to the Bible. We know that everything in the Bible is true. Pretty cool, huh? Just make sure that what you believe is in the Bible so that you can be sure that you believe in the truth.

187

Quiz 55

1. If someone believes something does that make it **true**? (Remember... the chocolate cake story...)

2. What does Numbers 23:19 say about God? What does it say that he will not do?

3. What is one book that is completely **true**?

4. What is one thing you learned from this section?

5. How are you going to apply what you learned today to your life?

Riddle Me This...

<u>Puzzle #1</u> – **DOT** DELIRIUM

Instructions for this game are found in Chapter 8, on page 71.

__ __ __ __   __ __ __ __ __ __ __

__ __ __ __   __ __ __ __ __ __

Go Read Proverbs 21 Again

Ok, this next verse is also very interesting:

> To do what is right and just is more acceptable to the LORD than sacrifice. Proverbs 21:3 NIV

Let me explain a bit more about the Bible. It is generally split up into a couple of major sections. We're going to be looking at the very first section, the Pentateuch (pent-uh-tuke - rhymes with mint-a-puke). That's a strange word, huh? The Pentateuch includes the very first five books of the Bible: *Genesis*, EXODUS, *Leviticus*, **Numbers**, and DEUTERONOMY. (Just so you know, anytime you see penta- in a word, it means five. For example, a pentagon is a shape that has five sides.) Anyway, the Pentateuch is also known as the books of law, because the Pentateuch was where God laid out all of His laws for the people of Israel. Now, if God uses five books of the Bible to give us all of these laws about sacrifice and different stuff, doesn't it kind of seem weird that there is something more important to him than sacrifice? But there is, because that is what the above verse says! Despite all of that time spent on teaching the people how to sacrifice for their sins, there is something that is *way* more important to God: our obedience and our hearts. Wow! God wants our obedience and our

Real Life

Give God your heart today! Pick a verse and obey it. Can't think of a verse? Well, here's one!

Children, obey your parents in everything, for this pleases the Lord.
—Colossians 3:20

hearts. He doesn't just want us to obey Him because we have to; He wants us to obey Him because of our love for Him. Carefully read this next verse:

> The sacrifice of an evil person is detestable, especially when it is offered with wrong motives. Proverbs 21:27 NLT

God really doesn't want us to offer Him our stuff instead of our hearts. He doesn't need anything; He just wants our hearts. That's why He hates the sacrifice of the wicked, because the wicked don't give Him their full hearts. If you're not already serving in your church, you should talk to your parents about starting pretty soon. If you already are serving in your church, make sure that you're doing it with a right heart. Don't stomp your feet and wear a frowny face. Do it joyfully, with a smile on your face. Give God your heart, not your actions.

Quiz 56

1. What is the Pentateuch? (Hint: Penta = 5)

2. What attitude does God want us to obey him with?

3. What attitude does God not want us to obey him with?

4. What is one thing you learned from this section?

5. How are you going to apply what you learned today to your life?

Riddle Me This...

Puzzle #2 – CROSSWORD CRAM

Across
3. To do what is right and just is more acceptable to the LORD than ___?___.
5. God wants our ___?___

Down
1. The first five books of the Bible
2. Give God your heart, not your ___?___
4. The kind of cake that your friend thinks she is eating

Pentateuch

Sacrifice

Chocolate

Hearts

Actions

Verse of **Fame**

Proverbs 21:31

The horse is made ready for the day of battle, but victory rests with the LORD.

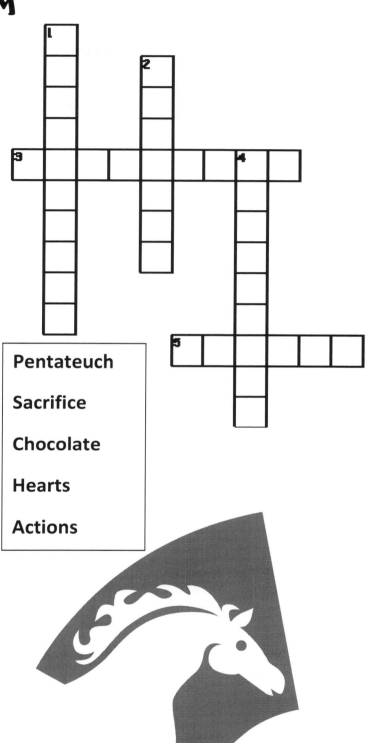

Go Read Proverbs 21 (yes, *again*)

Ok, let's look at a few more verses:

> *The violence of the wicked sweeps them away,*
> *because they refuse to do what is just. Proverbs 21:7 NLT*
>
> *The Righteous One takes note of the house of the wicked*
> *and brings the wicked to ruin. Proverbs 21:12 NIV*

Have you ever seen pictures of a town that has been flooded? There might have been houses that were floating, or flooded cars, or torn up trees, or broken signs. There is a special kind of flood called a flash flood. These floods often happen near the mountains. In a flash flood, a whole bunch of snow will melt very quickly and it will all come **rushing** down on a town. It tears up everything. It becomes like a gigantic broom that sweeps everything away. That's what will happen to the wicked. God says that their sins will cause disaster in their lives. Even though it seems like they're doing alright today, they could be dead and facing judgment tomorrow. Everyone who has sins will be swept away. That's why we need to hold onto Jesus, because He is the only One who can save us. Let's take a look at this last verse. "The Righteous One takes note of the house of the wicked." This verse is kind of saying, "God knows where you live!" Have you ever seen someone in a movie say, "I know where you live!"? What they are really saying is, "You can't hide from me!" You can't hide from God either. He can't be fooled. The wicked will be judged. Justice will be done. But **THANKFULLY**, God is our great Protector, and the Healer of our hearts. He sweeps away the wicked, but protects His children. Isn't that **cool**?

Quiz 57

1. What does the Bible compare God's wrath to?

2. Which one would God rather do: save us or **DESTROY** us?

3. Who does God **DESTROY**?

4. What is one thing you learned from this section?

5. How are you going to apply what you learned today to your life?

Puzzle #3- Code Crusher

Decoding directions contained in the letter... (just read the letter below)

They are swept away by their lack of insight

What the difference is between wrong and right

Their violence kills them, because they cannot see

This verse tells of the wicked, and their unjust deeds

Proverbs 21:___

SuperSpiesRUs.INC
321 SuperSneak Ln.
Hidden, Hiding 54321
1-800-ISPYONU

Top Secret
This Letter Permitted to
Authorized Personnel Only

Dear CodeCrusher:

We got an email from a random person with this attachment. They said that they were walking around downtown (right where I'm thinking one of their women spies lives), when suddenly this piece of paper fell from the sky. When the person looked up, they could just barely see someone walking away from the fifth story window of an apartment. Weird.

It seems like whoever lives in that apartment encoded a secret message. I hope you can crack the code.

Good Luck,
Mr. SuperSneaky

P.S. – These references were written on the back of the paper. I think that one of them is the answer to the puzzle. Circle the correct one. Hope you get it.

Proverbs 21:2   Proverbs 21:7

Proverbs 21:15   Proverbs 21:19

CHAPTER 22:

THOU BRAVE FOOTBALL PLAYER

Go Read Proverbs 22

Some **cool** things are in the next couple of chapters. Solomon splits up his sayings into thirty sayings that we can apply to our lives. Chapter 22 gives us the first six sayings, and we find the last of the sayings in Chapter 24. We'll get to those later. First, let's take a look at a couple of verses:

> *Choose a good reputation over great riches; being held in high esteem is better than silver or gold. Proverbs 22:1 NLT*

Real Life

Just because someone doesn't have the newest, coolest things doesn't mean that they can't be awesome friends. Give someone unpopular a chance today. Be a friend.

Many, many people will tell you that the most important thing that you can ever get is **money**. They will tell you that with **money**, you can rule the world. They say that you'll never have to work hard - you'll never have to worry about anything. Sounds pretty good, doesn't it? But have you seen that type of thinking throughout Proverbs? Have you seen God wanting his people to be the richest people in the world? It doesn't seem like **money** is really important to Him at all. Let's pretend that you're playing baseball, and you accidentally get hit in the head really, really hard with a flying baseball bat. At first, you see nothing but **blackness**; but then you find yourself in a dimly lit room. On one side of the room, you see this mountain of gold coins that fills up half of the room. But you also see a picture on a plain table on the other side of the room. The picture shows you wearing nice clothes and smiling. This picture represents your reputation. You hear a voice that says, **"BILLY, YOU MUST CHOOSE! WHICH ONE WILL YOU TAKE?"** What would you choose? I'm sure that right now you would say that you would pick your reputation. Let me ask you a question: Are you really making choices that protect your reputation, even if money is involved? If a friend promised you twenty bucks if you dropped a spider in your little sister's cup, would you pick your reputation over the twenty bucks? That's a pretty hard question. On some days, I would be tempted to throw the spider in her cup. Remember that your reputation affects God's reputation. You need to make choices that would be pleasing to God, and choices that reflect a good picture back on Him.

Check out this verse:

> *The rich and poor have this in common: the LORD made them both. Proverbs 22:2 NLT*

In your mind, who do you think is more pleasing to God? Does He find the little homeless boy who prays every day for help, or the rich boy who goes to church every week more pleasing? Would it surprise you that God sees them the same way? He loves them both! Do you love them both? Would you rather be seen playing basketball with the homeless boy, or be seen playing the Xbox® with the rich child? That's a hard question, isn't it? I think most of us would rather play Xbox® with the rich boy. We need to change this attitude. **Money** doesn't make a person better. It's all about what's on the inside.

Ok, let's check out the wise sayings. Since some Bibles don't have the sayings marked, I put in the references for you. Read the saying, and then read the little thought on it. Don't worry, there's only thirty! One more thing: I'm not going to write out most of the verses. This will give you guys more practice using your Bibles. Have fun!

Saying #1: Proverbs 22:17-21

The first saying of the wise is a plea to listen to wisdom. Pretty easy, right? Actually it is very, very difficult. Do you remember how hard it is to take correction? It can be very difficult because we have a lot of pride, and don't want to admit that we're in the wrong. If we can lay all of that aside, we can begin to grow in wisdom.

Quiz 58

1. A lot of people have a lot of **money** and *don't* have to work and stuff, but do they really have EVERYTHING they need?

2. Name one time when you made a choice that valued something else more than your reputation. What should you have done in that situation?

3. What keeps us from listening to correction? (Saying #1)

4. What is one thing you learned from this section?

5. How are you going to apply what you learned today to your life?

Riddle Me This...

<u>Puzzle #1</u> – *Anagram Master*

(The first letter is a bit darker.)

A TRUE POINT

– – – – – – – – – –

Verse
of
Fame

<u>Proverbs 22:6</u>
Start children off on the way they should go, and even when they are old they will not turn from it.

Saying #2: Proverbs 22:22-23

These verses deal with the POOR. Let's actually take a look at these verses:

> Do not exploit the poor because they are poor
> and do not crush the needy in court,
> for the LORD will take up their case
> and will exact life for life.
> Proverbs 22:22-23 NIV

People sometimes take advantage of the POOR. They think that the POOR are helpless. Often, these people will trap the POOR into tough places because of their helplessness. But the Lord says that He will defend them. That's pretty powerful when the Lord promises that He will defend your case.

Saying #3: Proverbs 22:24-25

We need to control our anger, don't we? Do you ever feel like your anger is a monster that you can't control? Kind of like the Incredible Hulk? You just feel like it will come out at any moment and take over your body. Well, you can actually take control of your anger. The best way to do that is to pray that God will take away your anger. Another thing that you could do is take a look at the friends you hang out with. Do they have control of their anger? If you hang out with people who have a bad tempers, they will totally influence your temper, and it will be harder than ever to control it. If you respond to someone in anger, there is a very good chance that you could seriously damage that relationship. From every point of view, controlling your anger is *always* a good idea.

Quiz 59

1. According to Matthew 7:12, how should you treat the POOR? (Saying #2)

2. What is the best way to get rid of your anger? (Saying #3)

3. What will happen if you hang out with people with bad tempers? (Saying #3)

4. What is one thing you learned from this section?

5. How are you going to apply what you learned today to your life?

Riddle Me This...

Puzzle #2 – JUMBLED PHRASE

LE T'SREV IEWT HESA YING STHA TWEH EAR D,SH
ALLW E?TH EFIR STSA YINGS AIDT OLIS TENTO WIS DOM,A
NDTH ESEC ONDS AYI NGSA IDTO STA NDU PFO RTH EPO OR.
DO N'TFO RGE TTH EWO RDSOFT HESE WIS ESAY IN GS!

Write the answer out here!

_____

_____

_____

_____

_____

Saying #4: Proverbs 22:26-27

Saying number four deals with taking up ᵴᴇᴄᴜʀⁱᵗʸ ꜰᴏʀ ᴀ ᴅᴇʙᵗ. **Do you remember when we talked about this in Chapter 6? If you don't remember what taking up** ᵴᴇᴄᴜʀⁱᵗʸ ꜰᴏʀ ᴀ ᴅᴇʙᵗ **is, you should go read that first part of Chapter 6 again (53-54). If you do remember what taking up security for a debt is, make sure that you don't get caught in that kind of trap. Stay as far away as you can from this situation.**

Saying #5: Proverbs 22:28

Back in biblical times, they used to use gigantic stones to set the boundaries between different properties and lands and stuff. The only reason someone would try to move these boundaries would be if they were trying to cheat someone. Solomon warns us not to do that. Why? Because we know that the Lord will see it. He will have a response to what we do. Remember? This is the beginning of wisdom!

BAD IDEA

Remember, taking ᵴᴇᴄᴜʀⁱᵗʸ ꜰᴏʀ ᴀ ᴅᴇʙᵗ **is *bad* idea. You'd be paying for something you don't even want or own! Make sure that you aren't putting yourself in danger for something that you don't care about.**

Saying #6: Proverbs 22:29

Do you play any sports, know an instrument (Guitar Hero doesn't count), sing, or run the PowerPoint for your church? Did you know that God wants us to be ᴇˣᴄᴇˡˡᴇⁿᵗ **in these** things? **If we do our job well, we will get recognized for it. Back in the old times, kings would have the best of everything. They would have the best cooks, the funniest jesters, the bravest knights, the best musicians, and, yes, I'm sure if football was around back then they would've had the best quarterbacks. It was an honor to serve in the court of the king. Well, if you do your job** ᵴᴋⁱˡˡꜰᵘˡˡʸ,

201

you will be honored for your work. Besides, you're already doing it
for the King of all Kings. So work to do it skillfully!

Quiz 60

1. This is a review question from Chapter 6! What should you do if you took
   up security for a debt? (Saying #4)

2. How is "moving someone's boundary stones" similar to stealing?
   (Saying #5)

3. How does 1 Corinthians 10:31 apply to Saying #6?

4. What is one thing you learned from this section?

5. How are you going to apply what you learned today to your life?

Puzzle #3– Code Crusher

Decoding directions contained in the letter… (just read the letter below)

SuperSpiesRUs.INC
321 SuperSneak Ln.
Hidden, Hiding 54321
1-800-ISPYONU

Top Secret
This Letter Permitted to
Authorized Personnel Only

Dear CodeCrusher:

I think you know what to do on this one. Although, I think that there might be some kind of hidden message in your result of this puzzle. Maybe it has something to do with that one paper with all the blanks, but I don't know.

Good Luck,

Mr. SuperSneaky

```
S  L  I  S  T  E  N  T  T  S
E  O  T  H  E  C  S  N  K  E
C  E  S  A  H  Y  E  I  I  I
U  N  G  E  S  L  L  A  N  R
R  D  A  T  L  L  H  D  E  D
I  T  Y  E  F  A  E  W  I  A
T  L  C  U  N  B  L  C  H  N
Y  X  L  G  T  A  N  G  E  U
E  L  E  Y  O  U  R  L  I  O
Y  R  F  E  E  N  O  T  S  B
```

Anger	Excellent
Boundaries	Security
Cheat	Skillfully
Debt	Stone

— — — — — — — —

— — — — — — — — —

— — — — — — — — —

— — — — — — — —

— — — — —

— — — — — — — —

— — — — —

— — — —

CHAPTER 23:

Look, Up in the Sky! Is it a Bird?

Is it a Plane? No, it's... Money?

Go Read: Proverbs 23

In this chapter, Solomon continues on with his wise sayings. So, we'll keep searching for more exciting treasures.

Saying #7: Proverbs 23:1-3

Do you ever go to someone's house and they serve your favorite meal of all time? It might be tempting to just eat as much **FOOD** as possible. That is exactly what this saying is warning you against. Don't take advantage of the situation (to take advantage of a situation means to not think about helping anyone but yourself). Be *polite*, but don't eat too much. There are two parts of this saying. Read Proverbs 23:3, so that you will remember it:

> *Do not desire his delicacies, for it is deceptive food.*
> *Proverbs 23:3 NASB*

This is saying, "Hey, don't crave the ways of the rich." It's better to live a humble and poor life rather than a rich and proud life.

Saying #8: Proverbs 23:4-5

Do you ever get jealous of your friend because of all his cool toys? Do you ever say something like, "If I only had the brand new Tiki Flame Thrower, I would finally be able to be like my friends." It's hard. **Computers**, iPoDS®, **Xboxes**®, **WIIS**®, CELL PHONES: they all can be tempting to you. They scream, "You can't be happy without us! You need us!" A lot of people scream back, "OK!" They start running after these things, but they are always just out of reach. Have you ever heard of a leprechaun? Leprechauns are make-believe creatures that like to collect gold and trick people. Leprechauns always hide their gold in a pot at the very end of a rainbow. People try to journey to the end of the rainbow in order to steal the leprechaun's pot of gold. Well, you probably already knew this, but rainbows are caused by the sunlight hitting MILLIONS of tiny water droplets in the air. You can never get to the end of the rainbow, because it always moves away from you, because you can only see rainbows from a distance. That means that you can never, **ever** get to that pot of gold. That's how all treasure is, whether it is iPods®, TV's, or gaming systems - they will always be out of reach if you chase after them. That's what this Proverb tells us. If you hunt down riches, you'll never get to them. If you do get them, they won't bring the happiness you thought they would.

Real Life

Whenever you find yourself wanting the newest iThing, pray instead, and ask God to help you be thankful for what you have.

Quiz 61

1. Which is better: a rich and proud life or a simple, humble life? (Saying #7)

2. Even though the answer to the last question was kind of **OBVIOUS**, which life are you living? What can you do to change? (Saying #7)

3. Some people drink too much alcohol, which is a bad idea. It starts out when they tell themselves, "I'll try just one drink, and then I'll stop." But once they have one, all they want is another. How is this like trying to buy all of the cool stuff like iPods and cell phones? (Saying #8)

4. What is one thing you learned from this section?

5. How are you going to apply what you learned today to your life?

Riddle Me This...

Puzzle #1 – **Hidden Message**

NEW PUZZLE!!! Here's what to do: read the story and, as you go, write down all the numbers <u>in the order they appear</u> in the top row of boxes. Then, use the code on the side to translate it into a hidden message!

My mom sent me to the store yesterday. She told me to get 6 loafs of bread and 1 big block of cheese. She said that we will need 12 stacks of 19 cups each. She said that 5 apple pies would feed everyone, although I told her that we would need at least 18. She laughed at me and told me that if I was *that* hungry, I could buy 9 pies. She said that we would need 3 of the small, cheap turkeys and 8 soda packs. She also told me to get 5 packs of paper plates. She said that each pack should have at least 19 plates in each. I got the stuff, and I just noticed that I forgot to get the bread!

| A- |
| C- ❸ |
| E- ❺ |
| F- ❻ |
| H- ❽ |
| I- ❾ |
| L- ⑫ |
| R- ⑱ |
| S- ⑲ |

6					////						
F					////						

Write the final answer here!

Remember that __ __ __ __ __   __ __ __ __ __ __ **lie.**

Saying #9: Proverbs 23:6-8

When you were younger, did you ever play at someone's house, and they wouldn't share a toy with you? When their mom found out about it, she probably made her child share the toy with you. Your friend probably stuck out his lower lip, **threw** the toy at you, and said, "I don't want to play anymore." That's the type of person that this saying is talking about. Don't hang out with those people, because they aren't thinking about you at all. They're only thinking about themselves. Make sure you are not like that. Again, when you share, serve, or do anything, do it with a right attitude.

Saying #10: Proverbs 23:9

Don't waste your words on people who won't listen. That can be extremely hard; especially if they are people that you care about. You just feel that you have to correct them. But this saying tells you not to waste your words on them because that's all that you'll be doing: wasting your words.

Who Knew?

Proverbs isn't the *only* book of the Bible with wise sayings. If you want more of these sayings of wisdom, check out the book of Ecclesiastes. It's full of wisdom!

Saying #11: Proverbs 23:10-11

This is kind of a repeat of saying #5. Don't try to cheat people, because as verse 11 says, "Their Defender is strong; He will take up their case against you." God is a God of justice. He won't let the guilty prevail. That is also cool for another reason. We know that when we are wronged, God will take our side.

Saying #12: Proverbs 23:12

Commit yourself to instruction; attune your ears to hear words of knowledge. Proverbs 23:12 NLT

We know what it means to commit ourselves to something. What does it mean to attune your ear to something? To attune something means to adjust it. When somebody says, "Hey, let's tune into Fox News," it means to adjust the TV to Fox News. Do you ever feel like it is hard to "attune" your ears to listen to wisdom? It can be very difficult to adjust your ears. Guess what the best thing to do is? Pray. Pray that God will help you adjust your ears so that you will listen to wisdom. He loves it when we come before Him humbly and ask Him for help.

Quiz 62

1. What should you do with a friend who never shares? (Saying #9)

2. Why is it hard to talk sense into the fool? (Saying #10)

3. What is the best way to attune your ear to wisdom? (Saying #12)

4. What is one thing you learned from this section?

5. How are you going to apply what you learned today to your life?

Riddle Me This...

Puzzle #2 – **THE GRAY GAME**

See the second game of Chapter 3 (page 32) for instructions.

SCIPLINDIE NAD WOMISD LOUDSH EB GNAIDE. DBA

_____ ____ _____ ____ _____ __ _____. _____

FLUINENCES NDA SKEDWNEICS HSLOUD EB AVIOEDD.

_____ _____ ____ _____ _____ __ _____.

Verse of Fame

Proverbs 23:13

Do not withhold discipline from a child; if you punish them with the rod, they will not die.

Saying #13: Proverbs: 23:13-14

This saying will become helpful when you become a **parent**, but it is also good to think through this stuff while you're a **kid**. You need to know that your parents aren't being unnecessarily cruel when they discipline you. They're doing it, because according to Proverbs, punishing you (and especially spanking you) will save you from death. So it is a good idea to accept discipline, because it is really saving your life.

Saying #14: Proverbs 23:15-16

Solomon is saying this to his son. But guess what? God says the same thing to us! God loves it when we gain wisdom. He loves hearing truth coming from our mouths, and He loves hearing us be just and fair. God is not super hard to please. He just wants your heart.

Saying #15: Proverbs 23:17-18

Remember when we talked about wishing that you were like the wicked person? Steer completely away from that. Always remember that their ways only lead to death.

Saying # 16: Proverbs 23:19-21

This saying warns us against hanging out with bad influences. These people are on their way to poverty. Look at that last verse again:

> *...For they are on their way to poverty.*
> *Too much sleep clothes a person with rags. Proverbs 23:21 NLT*

When you are **lazy**, poverty will overwhelm you. There's no doubt about it. You need to be diligent in your work, or someday you won't be able to support a family or even yourself. *Work hard* and you will do well. Besides, remember that when we are lazy, it reflects poorly on Christ. You need to protect His good reputation.

Quiz 63

1. What does God really want from you? (Saying #14)

2. The ways of the wicked lead to ___?___. (Saying #15)

3. When you are lazy, what is the result? (Saying #16)

4. What is one thing you learned from this section?

5. How are you going to apply what you learned today to your life?

Riddle Me This...

Match the truth on the right to the saying it goes to on the left. You might need to look back in the text for help.

1 •

2 •

3 •

4 •

5 •

6 •

7 •

8 •

9 •

10 •

11 •

12 •

13 •

14 •

15 •

16 •

- Don't cheat people because their defender is strong
- Don't hang out with bad influences
- Commit yourself to instruction
- Don't take up security for a debt
- Don't wish to be wicked.
- Parents discipline out of love
- Don't waste your words on non-listeners
- Give God your heart, not just your actions
- Have a servant's attitude
- Control your anger
- Don't take advantage of a situation
- Listen to wisdom
- Don't take advantage of the poor
- Be excellent at your talents
- Don't chase after false riches
- Don't cheat people

Saying #17: Proverbs 23:22-25

It's always a good idea to obey your **parents**. Remember how in Chapter 4 we looked at why older people are wiser than younger people? Well, that's one reason why we should listen to them, but it is also just a good idea to listen to your elders in general. Check out this verse from Colossians:

> *Children, always obey your parents, for this pleases the Lord.*
> *Colossians 3:20 NLT*

It's important for us to follow our **parents**. When we do, we are following God's will. We have seen plenty of times how this is always a good thing in our lives.

Saying #18: Proverbs 23:26-28

More of that adult stuff... when you are married, treasure your husband or wife, and never let anyone else hurt that special relationship. Enough said for now. Let's move on.

Saying #19: Proverbs 23:29-35

This is also aimed more at adults. Let's talk about it for a minute since you might be dealing with this stuff when you are a little older. This saying is talking about drinking too much alcohol. Now I know what you're thinking, "Me? **NEVER!**" I once heard this really great quote by Francis Chan, "Nobody becomes a drunk or a drug addict overnight". Ok, that's a pretty profound quote. It is saying that to get yourself in a dangerous situation, like being an alcoholic, it takes a series of choices. It might be tempting to take one more drink, but it would be very easy to let yourself get carried away. It could destroy you. If you fall for it, it will ruin your life. If you're attitude is, "I'll never, **ever** become an alcoholic..." GOOD! Keep it that way! But, if your attitude is like, "Oh, it can't be that dangerous," you're standing on the edge of a very slippery slope. The Bible clearly warns you to back away while you still can.

Good job! We only have one more section on these sayings. Well done. Remember these sayings, because they provide a good overview of Proverbs.

Quiz 64

1. Following God's will is always a good idea. So how should that help you want to obey your PARENTS?
   (Saying #17)

2. Pretend that you're trying to go down a mountain, and you suddenly slip on a rock. But after that rock you keep on slipping more and more. How is this like drinking too much and other bad influences? (Saying #18)

3. Why is it a bad idea to drink lots of beer? What's the danger? (Saying #18)

4. What is one thing you learned from this section?

5. How are you going to apply what you learned today to your life?

Puzzle #4 – Code Crusher

Decoding directions contained in the letter... (just read the letter below)

SuperSpiesRUs.INC
321 SuperSneak Ln.
Hidden, Hiding 54321
1-800-ISPYONU

Top Secret
This Letter Permitted to
Authorized Personnel Only

Dear CodeCrusher:

Well, this one might be a bit tough. I was following a guy from WidGeTS when this slip of paper fell from his purse...I mean bag. Sorry, it looked like a purse. Anyway, I think that all you need to do is shift the tiles around until they make a phrase. Easy, right? I figured out that the last word is "beer", and I wrote a note next to the first tile. Hope that helps.

Good Luck,
Mr. SuperSneaky

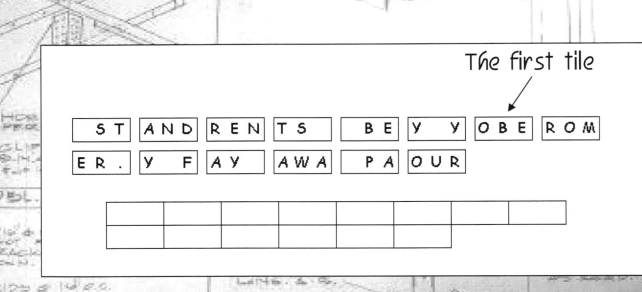

The first tile

CHAPTER 24:

Arise, Thou Lazy Couch Potatoeth

Go Read Proverbs 24

We have eleven more sayings of the wise to look at before we move on. Let's dive right in.

Saying #20: Proverbs 24:1-2

This saying is similar to saying #15. God doesn't want us to try to be like the wicked. He wants us to follow Him, and not run after things that only pretend to be as good as God. Also remember that the wicked always end up in a bad spot. We don't want to end up in that same spot! In fact, this verse tells to not even **hang** around them. God really wants us to have nothing to do with the wicked.

Saying #21: Proverbs 24:3-4

Ok, what does it mean when it says, "By wisdom a house is built?" I know you're sitting there thinking, "You can use wisdom like a nail?" No! God is teaching us how to build up our FAMILY. It's like saying, "You need wisdom to build a FAMILY, understanding to make it succeed, and knowledge to be able to provide your family with the stuff that they'll need." Pretty simple, right?

Saying #22: Proverbs 24:5-6

Ok, let's pretend that you're back in the Dark Ages and you are a knight. You're under the authority of a wise ruler. Pretend that this other nation keeps ATTACKING your king's people. Your king doesn't like that, so he decides to go to war with these people. Now, is he just going to grab a couple of his close friends and go to battle against his enemies? No, of course not! He's going to call EVERYONE in his kingdom who is able to fight. He's going to train different people to do specific jobs. *Then* he will go to battle. And while you're in battle, the king stays back behind the battle with his wisest advisors. Whenever something new happens in the battle, a knight will run back to the king to tell him what happened. Then the king can make a decision on how to fix the problem. Do you understand these verses?

Who Knew?

Where are the King's plans? Well, you were probably reading them a couple minutes ago! God wrote down all His plans in one big book... that's right. God's plans are in the Bible!

218

Ok, how can you apply this to your life? Well, you can remember to always think very, very carefully about what you are going to do. You might even get advice like the king did. If you do that, you are less likely to make a really dumb move.

Quiz 65

1. What does Saying #20 talk about?

2. What does Proverbs mean when it says, "By wisdom a house is built"? (Saying #21)

3. Name several people who can give you good advice. (Saying #22)

4. What is one thing you learned from this section?

5. How are you going to apply what you learned today to your life?

Riddle Me This...

Puzzle #1 – *MAZE MAYHEM*

You are Alex the knight. You have a huge army, and you are obeying the king, who told you to go on a very dangerous mission to fight another kingdom. After you get a lot of advice from the king, you set off. But can you get there?

Saying #23: Proverbs 24:7

Let's take a look at this verse:

> *Wisdom is too high for fools; in the assembly at the gate they must not open their mouths. Proverbs 24:7 NIV*

Wisdom is too high for fools? "Wow, fools must be really tiny." No, no, no. That's not it. It means that wisdom is too good for fools. It'd be like giving an iTouch™ to a baby. The baby doesn't know all the things an iTouch™ can do. All the baby knows is that it makes a big boom when he throws it at the floor. Of course WE know 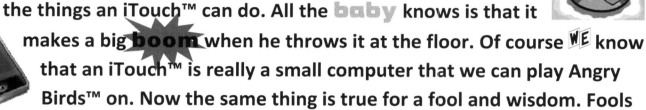 that an iTouch™ is really a small computer that we can play Angry Birds™ on. Now the same thing is true for a fool and wisdom. Fools don't see all of the cool stuff that wisdom can do for us. They just think that it only means to be smart. Yet, there is so much more to wisdom. It's not just being smart; it's making good and wise decisions. The fool also doesn't see the blessings that come from wisdom.

Saying #24: Proverbs 24:8-9

Schemers love to plot evil. They often think that their schemes will work out. But look at the second part of that verse. "The schemes of folly ARE sin." Do you remember what happens to the wicked? They will be swept away. The schemes of the wicked will never work out. They will only lead to disaster. Remember that.

Saying #25: Proverbs 24:10-12

Do you ever wish you were a SUPER hero, and that all you did all day was fly around with a cool cape and SAVE people? Well, God says that we need to be HEROES and SAVE people. What? Well, we have already looked at what happens when we sin. We go to hell to pay FOR our sins. But we also know that JESUS saved us from hell by paying for our sins. Jesus did that for everyone. Everyone who knows Jesus can go to Heaven. But not everyone knows about Jesus. SO guess what our job is? We need to be super heroes for God. We get to be his helpers and TELL PEOPLE all ABOUT Jesus. How cool is that? You're like GOD's super secret agent.

Quiz 66

1. What can the fool not see? (Saying #23)

2. "The schemes of folly are ___?___. (Saying #24)

3. Since Jesus died on the cross for us, what is our job? (Saying #25)

4. What is one thing you learned from this section?

5. How are you going to apply what you learned today to your life?

Riddle Me This...

Puzzle #2 – THE BOARD GAME

Instructions for this game are found in Chapter 3, on page 30.

__ __ __ __ __ __ _____,

__ __ __ __ ___.

Proverbs 24:26

An honest answer is like a kiss on the lips.

223

Saying #26: Proverbs 24:13-14

Do you like honey? I love honey. I even eat it on jellybean pizzas with salami. Just kidding. But, no, I do love honey. Did you know that just as much as you like honey, you should like wisdom? It should be like your favorite snack. You should crave wisdom.

Saying #27: Proverbs 24:15-16

Have you ever played with Weebles®? You know, those little toys that always stand upright. They can kind of get annoying. I'm the type of guy that likes to knock stuff over, and I never could knock over a Weeble®. I would have to stand it on its head. (Which only works if they have a flat head, which is very rarely.) But that's just not the same. That's how the righteous are. They're like Weebles®. They always get back up again. Do you ever feel like giving up? And you hate the, "if At fiRSt YOU dON't SUCCEEd tRY, tRY AGAiN" quote? Let me tell you that you can do it! Don't back down, or you are sure to fail! But if you try again, you have a chance to succeed. Brush yourself off, and get back in there. Take a quick look at this verse:

> *For though the righteous fall seven times, they rise again, but the wicked stumble when calamity strikes. Proverbs 24:16 NIV*

Think of yourself as a Weeble®. Remember that God wants you to save people. Well, Satan doesn't like that. The Bible says that we're in a spiritual war. Satan is trying to knock you down and get you to make wrong decisions in your life. Don't let yourself get taken out in the first battle. Hang in there.

Saying #28: Proverbs 24:17-18

> *Do not gloat when your enemy falls; when they stumble,*
> *do not let your heart rejoice,*
> *or the LORD will see and disapprove*
> *and turn His wrath away from them.*
> *Proverbs 24:17-18 NIV*

Do you know someone that you don't get along with very well? You wish that they would fall into a mud puddle or something. Well the Bible says that when something bad happens to those people, don't let yourself be happy. Have compassion. Jesus said that we need to love our enemies. You need to be careful and follow God's word carefully.

Quiz 67

1. In what way should we be like Weebles®? (Saying #27)

2. When Saul died, a messenger came and told King David. Now, if you're not familiar with the story, Saul and David were not necessarily BFF. They were actually kind of enemies. But instead of rejoicing when he heard that his enemy had been hurt, David tore his clothes in sorrow. So what should we not do when our enemies fall, even if it might be God's will? (Saying #28)

3. What should we do *instead* of being happy that our enemy has fallen? (Saying #28)

4. What is one thing you learned from this section?

5. How are you going to apply what you learned today to your life?

Riddle Me This...

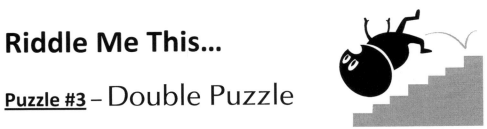

<u>**Puzzle #3**</u> – Double Puzzle

For though the __?__ fall seven times, they rise again...

___ ___ (○) ___ ___ ___ ___ ___ ___

Don't __?__ down when you are tested by the devil

___ ___ ___ (○)

Know also that wisdom is like __?__ for you

___ (○) ___ ___ ___

Have __?__ on your enemies (Honey)

___ ___ ___ ___ (○) ___ ___ ___ ___ ___

The LORD will see and disapprove

and turn His __?__ away from them.

___ ___ ___ (○) ___

| Honey |
| Fall |
| Compassion |
| Wrath |
| Righteous |

Don't ___ ___ ___ ___ ___ over your enemies.

Saying #29: Proverbs 24:19-20

Are you ever afraid that your house will get robbed or something? Maybe you're afraid of a bully at school? You don't need to be afraid. God is on your side and is fighting for you. God doesn't want us to live in fear, but to live trusting Him.

Saying #30: Proverbs 24:21

Have you ever seen people protesting on the news? They hold signs that say stuff like this: "Women are people too," "Down with the government," "Cut taxes."

Real Life

God not only wants us to obey the government, but He wants us to obey *all* authority. Submit to a parent or a teacher today. If you do, you'll feel really good!

People are always trying to change the government. They hate how their lives are currently going, and so they want to blame a lot of that on the GOVERNMENT. Some

people even blame stuff on God. "Uh, oh… I can see where this is going." Yeah. Guess what? Life generally doesn't go well for those people. Solomon is telling us not to join up with rebellious people, because you never know what is going to happen to them. Here is a very good example about staying away from protestors. One time, there was this man named *Korah* who didn't like God or Moses (he didn't like the GOVERNMENT of God). He was complaining and tried to lead a rebellion against Moses. As he was talking to Moses, God caused the earth to open up and swallow Korah and all of his followers. God then caused fire to fall from heaven to kill anyone with a rebellious attitude. Do you see why it's not a good idea to join those people? You never know what is going to happen to them. By the way, if you want to read that story about *Korah*, it is in Numbers 16. The next twelve verses in Proverbs

24 are more wise sayings. Read them, and see if you can figure out what they mean.

Quiz 68

1. Why should you not be afraid? (Saying#29)

2. Name one time when you were afraid and trusted God. (Saying #29)

3. Why should you not join troublemakers? (Saying #30)

4. What is one thing you learned from this section?

5. How are you going to apply what you learned today to your life?

Puzzle #4– *Code Crusher*

Decoding directions contained in the letter… (just read the letter below)

SuperSpiesRUs.INC
321 SuperSneak Ln.
Hidden, Hiding 54321
1-800-ISPYONU

Top Secret
This Letter Permitted to
Authorized Personnel Only

Dear CodeCrusher:

Well, this one seems to have been made by a kid spy, so it shouldn't be THAT hard. I think. We found the note on the sidewalk outside the school, and the teacher, who works for us, got a picture. Anyway, just follow the kid's instructions.

Good Luck,

Mr. SuperSneaky

Try to figure out my anagram

Now put the answer in here.
DON'T TEAM UP WITH

_ _ _ _ _ _ _ _ _ _ _ PEOPLE.

Have fun!

CHAPTER 25:

The Good, the BAD, and the Good That Became BAD

Go Read Proverbs 25

Ok, we're already at Chapter 25. But what's up with the very first verse in this chapter?

> These are more proverbs of Solomon, compiled by the men of Hezekiah king of Judah. Proverbs 25:1 NIV

Who was Hezekiah? Well, let's take a look at that. Keep in mind that he's not an author of Proverbs. It's time to look at a little bit of Israelite history. Solomon had 1000 wives. A lot of these women were from many different nations and most of them didn't believe in the true God. They caused Solomon to turn away from God. God wasn't too happy, but He had promised David that nothing bad would happen to Solomon. So *after* Solomon's death, God split up Israel into two parts: Israel and Judah. He allowed other *kings* to control most of Israel, but he let *King* David's family rule over the tribe of Judah. Often the *kings* of

Who Knew?

Hezekiah was the son of Ahaz, a bad king of Judah. Yet he still did what was right when he grew up. That's pretty cool!

Judah didn't follow God as they should have (though there were both good and bad *kings*). Israel never fully regained its glory because of what Solomon did.

Hezekiah was one of the good *kings* of Judah. Look at these verses about him:

> Hezekiah trusted in the LORD, the God of Israel. There was no one like him among all the kings of Judah, either before him or after him.
> He held fast to the LORD and did not stop following Him;
> he kept the commands the LORD had given Moses.
> 2 Kings 18:5-6 NIV

Pretty cool, huh? Because Judah was kind of a mess, a lot of the original writings of Solomon disappeared. They even lost their Bible for a long time! One of the things that Hezekiah did during his rule was to have his men look for the writings of Solomon. Proverbs 25-29 is the stuff that they found. Wow!

Quiz 69

1. Who caused Solomon to turn away from God?

2. Who was Hezekiah?

3. What did Hezekiah have his men do about Solomon's *missing* Proverbs?

4. What is one thing you learned from this section?

5. How are you going to apply what you learned today to your life?

Riddle Me This...

Puzzle #1 - CROSSWORD CRAM

Use the hints to find the answers for the crossword below.

Across →

2. What happened to the original scrolls of the Bible? They __?__.

4. The job that Solomon, David, and Hezekiah all had

5. What tribe were David, Solomon, and Hezekiah from?

6. The thing that lead King Solomon away from God

Down ↓

1. The good king that found Proverbs 25

3. Hezekiah ___?___ in the Lord

Hezekiah
Judah
Wives
King
Trusted
Disappeared

Go Read Proverbs 25 Again

Let's take a look at some of these verses.

> If you find honey, eat just enough—too much of it, and you will vomit.
> Seldom set foot in your neighbor's house—too much of you,
> and they will hate you. Proverbs 25:16-17 NIV

Do you like honey? Or maybe candy? How about cake? Or ice cream? All of this stuff is really good. Do you ever feel like you could just eat that stuff forever and ever? You are sure that you'll never get SICK despite your parents always saying, "If you eat too much junk food, you'll get SICK and DIE!" Well, you might not die, but you can definitely get *way* SICK. I know you're thinking, "Yeah right!" I used to think that too... until I died. Just kidding. Ok, why is Proverbs telling us something that our parents tell us all of the time? Proverbs is giving you an example. Sure, if you eat a ton of honey, you will get SICK. But too much of anything isn't good (except for God). Here's another example that will help you understand: Pretend that you like some music that is really, really cool. You especially like this one song; you play it over, and over, and over, and over, and over, and over, and, over again. (I've done that with a lot of my music.) After you have listened to it a bazillion times, you find that you really, really don't like that song anymore. So it is very possible to have too much of a good thing.

Let's take a look at that second verse. Do you have a friend's house that you love to play at? Or maybe you have a friend that loves to come over to your house all of the time. Have you ever known someone who comes over to your house everyday for, like, three weeks? You find yourself getting pretty SICK of them. You soon focus on everything that bugs you about them. That's what this verse is saying. If you want to keep your friends, then give them some space. You don't need to be at their house all of the time.

Quiz 70

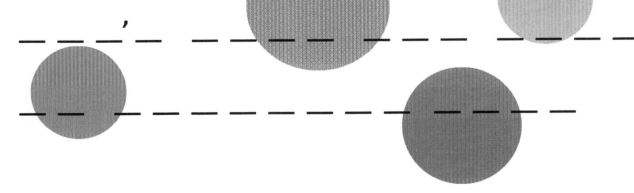

1. Is it possible to have too much of a good thing? Give me an example.

2. If you're around somebody for too long, they can get annoying. So what should you do to keep your friendships positive?

3. What is the one thing that you can never have enough of?

4. What is one thing you learned from this section?

5. How are you going to apply what you learned today to your life?

Riddle Me This...

Puzzle #2– **DOT** DELIRIUM

Instructions for this game are found in Chapter 8, on page 71.

_ _ _ ' _ _ _ _ _ _ _ _ _ _

_ _ _ _ _ _ _ _ _ _ _ _ _

Go Read Proverbs 25 (yes, *again*)

Alright gang, check out these verses:

> *Like one who takes away a garment on a cold day, or like vinegar poured on a wound, is one who sings songs to a heavy heart. Proverbs 25:20 NIV*
>
> *Like a muddied spring or a polluted well are the righteous who give way to the wicked. Proverbs 25:26 NIV*

Have you ever been angry, upset, or extremely sad? Like maybe when your pet died. And your friend bounces up and says, "Hey, Alex, what happened when the chicken did the splits in gym class?" Your pet just died. You're not in any mood to listen to a silly chicken JOKE. Did you like that friend very much right then? You probably got upset with them, didn't you? Sometimes, when someone is having a really hard time, someone will try to "lighten the mood" by telling a JOKE, or by trying to be funny. Sometimes, there is no "lightening the mood". When you see a friend who is having a really, really hard time, just try to be there for them. Instead of trying to lighten the mood, join them in their sorrow. That is often the most caring thing that you can do for them.

BAD IDEA

Don't be disrespectful! When your friends are hurting, make sure that you don't try to lighten the mood. Try to understand what they are going through.

What about that second verse? Back in biblical times, water was very important. People would build their cities near wells, so that the city would have plenty of water. Where there was water, things would grow. Whenever water went bad in a certain area (like maybe by pollution or poison) things would die. Have you ever been playing at the beach, and the water was *crystal* clear?

Then a whole bunch of people came into the water and stirred up the mud. The water can start to look disgusting very quickly. Or have you ever gone to a public swimming pool and the water was clean until a whole bunch of people got in the water at the same time (EWW!)? That's what it is like when the righteous give way to the wicked. They become disgusting. They only bring death everywhere they go, and nobody wants to be around them. That's why it's important to watch what things influence you. You don't want to end up being like dirty beach water! Instead, you want to be life giving water. You want to bring life wherever you go. Not death. You want to be that good well that the city is built around.

Rewrite the poem here

1._____

_____

2._____

_____

3._____

_____

4._____

_____

5._____

_____

6._____

_____

7._____

_____

- Proverbs 25:6

- Proverbs 25:17

- Proverbs 25:25

- Proverbs 25:26

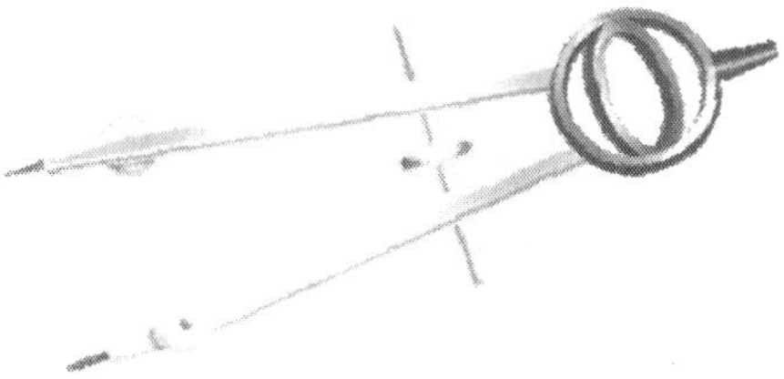

CHAPTER 26:

  Rocks, PATRIOTIC Snowmen,

and a Loud-Mouthed Fool

Go Read Proverbs 26

Chapters 26-29 all contain more maxims that *King* Hezekiah's men found. Isn't that cool? There are a lot of verses here that are talking about the ꜰᴏᴏʟɪsʜ man. Let's take a close look at this, because we can learn a lot from looking at a ꜰᴏᴏʟ. Remember that if some of this applies to you, change your life! Pray that God will help you. You don't want to end up like that dirty pool water from Chapter 25!

Let's take a look at the very first verse that we see in Proverbs 26:

> *Like snow in summer or rain in harvest,*
> *honor is not fitting for a fool. Proverbs 26:1 NIV*

Have you ever gone to a Fourth of July parade and, all of the sudden, it starts to snow very hard during the middle of it? Pretty soon you're building snowmen and having snowball fights and

you're just having the time of your life. But wait a second... snow on the Fourth of July? Something doesn't seem right. It never snows in July! That's what it's like to honor a fool. It doesn't make sense. ꜰᴏᴏʟs are not people to be admired; they're people that should be avoided!

That's what this verse is saying. Just like if you got snow during summer (which doesn't fit), it makes no sense to give honor to a fool. It just doesn't fit.

Quiz 72

1. What does "not fitting" mean?

2. Giving *glory* to fools is not fitting. Why not?

3. What should you do to fools so that their foolishness doesn't RUB off on you?

4. What is one thing you learned from this section?

5. How are you going to apply what you learned today to your life?

Riddle Me This...

Puzzle #1 – JUMBLED PHRASE

Ma n,its eem stha tgiv ingh ono rtoa fo olis pre tty,w ell, f ooli sh.i twou ldb e lik egettingh otco coaon awar mda y.Ori twou ldb elik eget tinga priz eeve ntho ughyo ulos tth era ce.t hin kabo uti t.

_____

_____

_____

_____

_____

_____

_____

Verse of **Fame**

Proverbs 26:11
As a dog returns to its vomit, so fools repeat their folly.

Go Read Proverbs 26 Again

Ok, Proverbs 26:4-5 are very interesting. Let's see why:

> *Do not answer a fool according to his folly,*
> *or you yourself will be just like him.*
> *Answer a fool according to his folly,*
> *or he will be wise in his own eyes.*
> *Proverbs 26:4-5 NIV*

The first verse tells us not to answer a fool according to his folly so that we won't be like him ourselves. But the second verse tells us to answer a fool according to his folly so that he doesn't think himself wise in his own eyes. Now it sounds like the Bible is CONTRADICTING itself here (CONTRADICTING means saying the opposite of what something else says). There are a lot of people today that will say something like, "Oh, I don't believe in the Bible because it is full of CONTRADICTIONS." This appears to be one of those CONTRADICTIONS. But if we take a closer look, we find that it really does make sense after all. There are a lot of things that are like that in the Bible. At first, they make no sense. But when

BAD IDEA

Whenever someone says something bad about the Bible, don't just take their word for it. If you look closer or ask a parent, many times you'll find that the person who said the bad thing didn't really know what they were talking about. In the end, the Bible will always win.

we look at them closely, they really do make sense. So, let's study this one. Ok, let's say you get in an argument with a loudmouthed ғοοʟ. He says something like, "You're so dumb for believing in God!" And so you say something like, "Well, you're dumb for not believing in God!" Who looks like a ғοοʟ there? You both do. Ok, that's what happens when you answer a ғοοʟ according to his

243

folly. Now let's rewind. He says, "You're so dumb for believing in God!" You don't say anything, and just look at your toes. *Now* who looks like a fool? YOU DO! He's going to think, "Oh, he can't even defend himself!" Are you confused yet? You should be. Basically, a ᶠOOL is a fool, and sometimes it is a very fine line between handling a ᶠOOL in a good way and handling him in a bad way. Maybe this verse will help you understand this:

> *But in your hearts revere Christ as Lord. Always be prepared to give an answer to everyone who asks you to give the reason for the hope that you have. But do this with gentleness and respect... 1 Peter 3:15 NIV*

The first part kind of says to make sure that you know that Christ is the king of your heart. Then it says to make sure that you have answers for everything that you believe, so that you have an answer for everyone who asks you about your faith. But get this: you're supposed to answer them with gentleness and respect.

Quiz 73

1. What does CONTRADICTING mean?

2. Is the Bible full of CONTRADICTIONS?

3. How should we answer someone who is questioning our faith? (Talk about your answer with your parents.)

4. What is one thing you learned from this section?

5. How are you going to apply what you learned today to your life?

Riddle Me This...

<u>Puzzle #2</u> – **Wordsearch Wackiness**

B	D	E	P	P	R	E	A
P	T	N	R	A	R	E	N
D	C	T	E	O	G	I	S
V	E	E	P	F	A	N	W
A	P	N	A	S	E	W	E
E	S	R	R	T	O	D	R
H	E	Z	E	K	I	A	H
A	R	N	D	Y	O	N	E

Answer   Respect

Prepared   Hezekiah

Defend

— —

— — — — — — —

— — — — — —

— — — — — — — —

— — — — — — — —

245

Go Read Proverbs 26 (yes, *again*)

Let's continue looking at how to respond to ᖴOOLs.

> *A gentle answer turns away wrath, but a harsh word stirs up anger. Proverbs 15:1 NASB or NIV*

Now that we've read these verses, let's rewind again and take a look at that first scene one last time. The guy says, "You're so dumb for believing in God!" And let's say that you say something like this, "Well, sir, you have some very interesting thoughts, but I have found proof that shows that there is a God and that *Christianity* is true; I believe that there is enough evidence to believe in both God and *Christianity*." Do you see how that's totally different? You began with respect and presented your case with *gentleness* (1 Peter 3:15). You've left him doubting his own wisdom, and you haven't made yourself look dumb.

Real Life

You should always give a gentle answer – even today. When someone irritates you today, answer them gently, and it will go much better for you.

Jesus said that the Holy Spirit will show you what to say at the exact right time in situations like this. In everything you say, think before you say it.

Always respond with respect and *gentleness*. If you do this, life will go a lot better for you.

Let's look at this last verse:

> *Whoever digs a pit will fall into it; if someone rolls a stone, it will roll back on them. Proverbs 26:27 NIV*

This is just reminding you that when you try to harm others, you'll only end up harming yourelf and that God takes up the case of the poor and helpless. He always sees to it that justice is done. So make sure that you never try to harm another person, because in the end, it will never turn out well for you.

Quiz 74

1. Name one time when you gave a gentle answer that turned away anger.

2. Name one time when you said a harsh words that stirred up anger.

3. What will happen if you try to harm others?

4. What is one thing you learned from this section?

5. How are you going to apply what you learned today to your life?

247

Puzzle #3– *Code Crusher*

Decoding directions contained in the letter... (just read the letter below)

SuperSpiesRUs.INC
321 SuperSneak Ln.
Hidden, Hiding 54321
1-800-ISPYONU

CONFIDENTIAL

Top Secret
This Letter Permitted to
Authorized Personnel Only

Dear CodeCrusher:

Here's our latest catch. I thought that it looked fishy (especially because Valentine's Day has already passed...). Anyway, I went ahead and opened it, and look what I found. HideNSeek is one of their trickiest spies. I've been trying to catch her for a long time. Well, you know what to do. Read her letter, and then unscramble her code. I'm too busy dusting the envelope (the one in the picture) for fingerprints.

Good Luck,
Mr. SuperSneaky

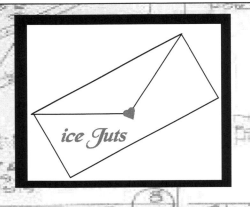

ice Juts

---

ice Juts

___ ___ ___ ___ ___ ___ ___

- Proverbs 26:1
- Proverbs 26:13
- Proverbs 26:22
- Proverbs 26:27

Dear Codemaker,

I hope that this helps. I hid it as a valentine. The only issue is that it isn't anywhere near Valentine's Day. Oh well. I hope that it gets through. Unscramble the anagram. The answer will tell you one thing that God is like. He always sees that this is done. I am giving you four verse references to help you find the verse that this key word belongs to. The verse is an example of how the answer is done. Well, I've got to go hide. That SuperSneakFreak is after me again.

Have fun!
HideNSeek

CHAPTER 27: FRIENDS FRIED TRUE

Go Read Proverbs 27

Today we're going to take a look at what it means to be a true friend. There is some really important stuff that we are going to be looking at, so pay close attention so that you don't miss it. Before we even begin, look at this verse:

> Be wise, my child, and make my heart glad. Then I will be able to answer my critics. Proverbs 27:11 NLT

What is SOLOMON saying? He is saying that whenever you do something, you might get criticized (you know, when someone's like, "Don't do it *that* way..."), no matter what it is. I'm sure that Solomon got a lot of criticism as a king. Sometimes, even God is criticized by people! But

Who Knew?

Did you ever notice that a lot of older people don't get criticized very much? It's because a lot of old people are wise (Chapter 4). Sometimes, the wiser you are, the less you get criticized.

SOLOMON was kind of saying, "Hey, be wise so that nobody can ever say that my words aren't right." Unfortunately for SOLOMON, he didn't live a very wise life, and neither did his son. But God is saying the exact same thing to us. He wants to be able to point at us and say, "My ways work! Just take a look at little Johnny and Jenny! They both live in my will and look how well their life is going for them!" Do you live that way? Job (pronounced "Jobe") did. God told *Satan* to take a look at Job because he was such a good guy. Check out what God says here:

> "Then the LORD said to Satan, "Have you noticed My servant Job? No one else on earth is like him. He is an honest and innocent man, honoring God and staying away from evil. You caused Me to ruin him for no good reason, but he continues to be without blame."
> Job 2:3 NCV

Can God say that about you? He wants you to live that way: "honoring God and staying away from evil." I know that it sounds incredibly **hard**. Just imagine trying to live a life that is so pleasing to God that He says, "Hey, check out that guy. Yup, that's My son!" If you follow the things that you've learned in Proverbs, you will be taking a giant step in that direction. So focus on obeying Him.

Quiz 75

1. How should we respond to criticism? (1 Peter 3:15)

2. Again, in this chapter, we see how your reputation reflects on your parents. How is this different than last time?

3. What are some ways that we can please God so that we can be like Job?

4. What is one thing you learned from this section?

5. How are you going to apply what you learned today to your life?

Riddle Me This...

Puzzle #1 – **Block Brain**

Unscramble the tiles to reveal a hidden message. The arrow points to the first tile.

O ON	ITIC	N CR	R LI	LIVE	E CA
AT N	FE S	YOU	O TH	IZE	YOU.

Verse
of
Fame

Proverbs 27:14
If anyone loudly blesses their neighbor early in the morning, it will be taken as a curse.

251

Go Read Proverbs 27 Again

Ok, let's take a look at how to be a good friend. Let's start with these verses.

> *Wounds from a sincere friend are better than many kisses from an enemy. Proverbs 27:6 NLT*
>
> *The heartfelt counsel of a friend is as sweet as perfume and incense. Proverbs 27:9 NLT*

We've talked a lot about accepting correction. We all know that sometimes correction can be offensive and even painful. The person who is willing to be honest with you is a true friend. Let's say that you saw a dog playing near the edge of the street. Now if you were a true friend to that dog, you would probably pull it away from the street so that it wouldn't get hurt. However, if you didn't know a lot about dogs, or you were scared of them, you probably wouldn't do anything to help it. Sometimes you can be right at the edge of a cliff and not know it. If someone truly loves you, they'll help pull you away from the edge, even if you

don't want help. Someone who isn't your friend probably won't bother. So if you ever get correction from someone, know that they aren't being mean, but it's because they love you. If you remember that, you'll be able to accept correction more easily.

Now look at that second verse. What does it say that the counsel from a friend is? Like *perfume*! You should love counsel from your friends because they're only trying to help you. Now, it might not seem that your friend's correction is a *perfume* at the time. In fact, sometimes it might even seem more like a wound than *perfume*. But, in the end, after you've seen what that correction saved you from, you will realize that it was more like a *perfume* than a wound. So take correction from your friends, because they're only doing it for your benefit. If you want to be a good friend, make sure that you are completely honest with your friends. Save them from destruction. That is the best way to be a true friend.

Quiz 76

1. Pretend that you keep on stealing chocolate candy from your mom's secret chocolate stash. A friend comes up and says, "Hey, Bobby, I heard that you were stealing candy, and I think that God might want you to stop." Do you think that he is being a good friend? Why or why not?

2. What is one way that you can tell that you have a good friend?

3. What do you have to be willing to do to be a good friend?

4. What is one thing you learned from this section?

5. How are you going to apply what you learned today to your life?

Riddle Me This...

<u>**Puzzle #2**</u> – Sanity Cipher

$$\times\ +\ =\ -\ \times$$

_ _ _ _ _

$$\gamma \leqslant +\ +\ \mu\ \gamma \times \Delta \leqslant \circ$$

_ _ _ _ _ _ _ _ _ _

$$\pi + \leqslant \leqslant\ \ \alpha$$

_ _ _ _ \ _

$$\pi + \Delta\ \mu\ \circ\ \delta$$

_ _ _ _ _ _

A	α
C	γ
D	δ
E	μ
F	π
I	Δ
M	$\leq$
N	$\circ$
O	$\leqslant$
R	$+$
S	$-$
T	$\times$
U	$=$

254

Go Read Proverbs 27 (yes, *again*)

Ok, let's keep rolling. Check out this cool verse:

> *As iron sharpens iron, so a friend sharpens a friend.*
> *Proverbs 27:17 NLT*

Now we're going to be talking about *KNIVES* (this is a great book for kids). Ok, when people sharpen *KNIVES*, they take a hard material (like a stone) with metals in it and scrape the edge of a *KNIFE* against it in order to sharpen it. Sometimes they'll make that stone into the shape of a wheel, and spin the wheel extremely fast. Then they'll take the edge of the *KNIFE* and lay it against the wheel so that it will sharpen it. That's how it should be with your friends. Without sharpening a *KNIFE*, it becomes pretty useless very quickly. So it's important that you have friends who will sharpen you – like a friend who helps you grow in Christ. Maybe they point out areas in your life that need some adjusting or they

Real Life

Not only should you find friends who sharpen you, but you should sharpen your friends. So help your friend today.

might tell you how important it is to obey the Bible. Thinking back to the *KNIFE* example, do you think that the *KNIFE* likes to be sharpened? No, because, when it is sharpened, the dull parts get scraped off of it. I bet that would hurt! But in the end, the knife is sharper and much better. So in your relationship with your family and friends, whenever they give you correction, they are sharpening you so that you will be a lot more effective. Place yourself in a position where you are consistently being sharpened by your friends and family, and you are consistently sharpening them. One of the best ways to do this is to make sure you have good, Christian friends who love Jesus. You will find that having good friends is one of the best thing you will ever do.

Quiz 77

1. If you were a knife, then you would notice that when someone sharpened you, little parts of you would get scraped off and it would be very painful. How is this similar to receiving correction?

2. Are you the kind of friend who sharpens others? What can you do to become more like that kind of friend?

3. What kind of friends do you need in order to be sharpened by them?

4. What is one thing you learned from this section?

5. How are you going to apply what you learned today to your life?

Puzzle #3- *Code Crusher*

Decoding directions contained in the letter... (just read the letter below)

SuperSpiesRUs.INC
321 SuperSneak Ln.
Hidden, Hiding 54321
1-800-ISPYONU

Top Secret
This Letter Permitted to
Authorized Personnel Only

Dear CodeCrusher:

Well, we had a spy (Shawna Sneekee) pick up this flyer that was hanging on that apartment door where I found the last code. I think there's something fishy about it. What's up with all the blanks? I don't know, but it might help if you read the fine print below.

Good Luck,

Mr. SuperSneaky

---

cALLING ALL RoADrUNNErS! THIS IS YOUR COMPLeTION POINT! cOME! ANY OF YOU WHO WANt TO RACE THE RABBiT CAN CoME TO MULBERRY STREET TO RACE! nOBODY sHoULD STAY HOme! time TO SHOW THE RABBIT WHO Is BOSS! huRRAY FOr tHE ROADRUNNERs!

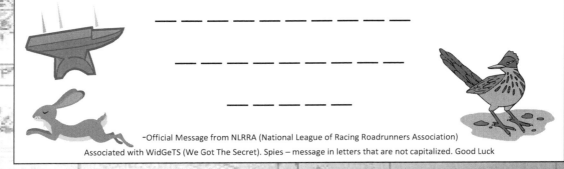

__ _ _ _ _ _ _ _ _ _ _

_ _ _ _ _ _ _ _ _

_ _ _ _ _

-Official Message from NLRRA (National League of Racing Roadrunners Association)
Associated with WidGeTS (We Got The Secret). Spies – message in letters that are not capitalized. Good Luck

CHAPTER 28:

MONEY, MONEY, MONEY

Go Read Proverbs 28

Money: IT's the thing that our whole world revolves around. People love money. They feel like they can't get enough of it. We've already seen some of the warnings against loving money, but we should take a closer look. BEfore we do, though, I want you to look at thIS verse:

> "No one can serve two masters. Either you will hate the one AND love the other, or you will be devoted to the one and despise the other. You cannot serve both God and money. Matthew 6:24 NIV

Real Life

When you find yourself loving money, pray and tell God how much more you love Him than money.

First of all, what does it mean to *love* money? I mean, we don't go around kissing money. Do you remember those Easter eggs from Chapter 2? This is the same thing. We *love* the stuff that we can get with money. We *love* the security about money that says, "If you have enough of me, you don't need anything else in this world." Isn't that kind of what God tells us? God promises that when we have Him, we really don't need anything else. It's like God versus Money. Which one will you follow? Now some people think, "Oh, I don't *love* my stuff that much. And besides, I can *love* my money and still *love* God." The verse that we just looked at says that you can't have **both/and**. You have to have **either/or**. You can't have **both** God **and** money; you have to pick **either** God **or** money. So let's take a look at this stuff.

Go Read Proverbs 28:1-8

Alright guys, check out these two verses:

> It is BETTER to be poor and innocent THAN to be rich and WICKED. Proverbs 28:6 NCV
>
> Some people get rich by overcharging others, but their wealth will be given to those who are kind to the poor. Proverbs 28:8 NCV

Do you remember how we looked at whether or not you would pick your reputation over RICHes? Well, this is almost the same situation. Would you choose riches or innocence? Now many, many people would say, "Whoa, whoa, whoa! Wait! You can be rich and INNOCENT at the same time!" Can't you? Well, let's THINK about this. What happens when you become rich? You have the whole world at your fingertips, don't you? Anything you say goes. But what can happen? You can easily be overcome by greed. You want everything, no matter what it may cost you. Now, I know that not all people are like this, but it can be very easy TO get swept away by your riches AND greed. When dealing with this type of stuff, the best thing to be is content with what you have. Now, I'm not telling you to go live in a cardboard box, but use what you have to bless other people and choose to be content with what you have.

Check out that second verse. What will happen to the money of people who get it wrongly? It will be given away to someone who will use it right! I know you're thinking, "I'll use it correctly! I love the POOR!" Nice try. Don't even think about

259

trying to get rich the wrong way. It's hard enough just following Jesus while you're rich, but it's impossible if you got those riches the wrong way. Be honest! If you live in a way that God wants you to, you won't have to worry about it.

Quiz 78

1. Is it possible to *love* both God and money?

2. What does it mean to *love* money?

3. What are some things that you can *love* instead of money?

4. What is one thing you learned from this section?

5. How are you going to apply what you learned today to your life?

Riddle Me This...

<u>Puzzle #1</u> – THE BOARD GAME

Instructions for this game are found in Chapter 3, on page 30.

___ ___ _____ ____ ___ _____ _____
 1   3   5   10   2   12   11

_____ _____ _____ ____ _____.
    9   6   8   4   7

Verse of Fame

<u>Proverbs 28:1</u>

The wicked flee though no one pursues, but the righteous are as bold as a lion.

Go Read Proverbs 28:9-19

Let's move on:

> *The rich are wise in their own eyes; one who is poor and discerning sees how deluded they are. Proverbs 28:11 NIV*

Ok, who is generally wise in his own eyes? Well, we know that whoever doesn't listen to correction thinks that that he is wise in his own eyes. "What? No he doesn't!" Ok, seriously think about this. What is the only reason someone doesn't listen to instruction? He thinks that he doesn't need it, right? So he thinks that he is doing just fine, that he is "wise enough." Well, we know that we all need correction sometimes. It's what makes us wise. Look at this verse from Proverbs 26:

> *Do you see a man who is wise in his own eyes?*
> *There is more hope for a fool than for him.*
> *Proverbs 26:12 ESV*

Wow! There is more hope for a fool than for someone who thinks that he is wise in his own eyes! That's some pretty serious stuff! We've seen the benefits of being wise and the horrors of being a fool and wicked. So again, if you are rich, be very careful that you keep a humble heart towards God and instruction. If you manage your heart and your riches in a way that is honoring to God, He will be pleased.

Quiz 79

1. What does "being wise in your own eyes" mean?

2. What person is worse off than a fool?

3. If you are rich, what is one thing that you should definitely do?

Study Up!

Give some other names for someone who is wise in their own eyes.

_____

_____

Why do *you* think that God doesn't want us to be wise in our own eyes?

_____

_____

4. What is one thing you learned from this section?

5. How are you going to apply what you learned today to your life?

Riddle Me This...

Puzzle #2 – **Falling Phrases**

Follow the instructions and finish the sentence:

1. Change the second letter of the word "Money" into the fifth letter in the alphabet.
2. Change the last letter into the (11+8)th letter in the alphabet.
3. Swap the 3rd and 4th letters. (Make sure they are both lowercase.)
4. Flip the 4th letter upside down.
5. Change the third letter into the last letter of the word you just wrote.
6. Change the first letter into the one that comes three before it in the alphabet

Money

1.

2.

3.

4.

5.

6.

INSTEAD OF LOVING MONEY, LOVE _____

Go Read Proverbs 28:20-28

We should look at one more verse about **riches**:

> *A faithful person will be richly blessed, but one eager to get rich will not go unpunished. Proverbs 28:20 NIV*

OK, in all this, it might seem tempting to want to get as much **money** as fast as you can. God promises that if you are faithful, He will be faithful to **richly** bless you – even though sometimes it might not be in the form of money. You just need to trust Him, because God's blessing is far better than all the **money** in the world. Let's look at one more verse:

> *Happy is the man who is always reverent, But he who hardens his heart will fall into calamity* [trouble]. *Proverbs 28:14 NIV*

Do you still **tremble** before God? God wants us to treat him like our daddy. He wants us to come before him with everything that bugs us and lay it down. He wants our hearts to be tender toward Him. If we do this, we will be blessed. God wants our hearts. If we don't do this, we will fall into trouble. Always keep your heart tender toward God, because if you're not in a good spot with God, it's impossible to do any of what you've learned so far.

Quiz 80

1. A person who is eager to get **rich** will _____?_____. (Proverbs 28:20)

2. What will happen if our hearts are not tender toward God?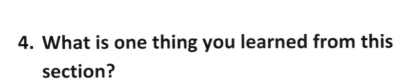

3. God wants us to treat him as if He we were our ___?___.

4. What is one thing you learned from this section?

5. How are you going to apply what you learned today to your life?

Puzzle #3- *Code Crusher*

Decoding directions contained in the letter... (just read the letter below)

SuperSpiesRUs.INC
321 SuperSneak Ln.
Hidden, Hiding 54321
1-800-ISPYONU

Top Secret
This Letter Permitted to
Authorized Personnel Only

CONFIDENTIAL

Dear CodeCrusher:

HideNSeek has been at it again with CodeCrusher. This time, CodeMaker left her a rebus to take it to their headquarters. I listened in on a phone call that was made by them later. Boy, was she mad that we had made it to the rebus and got it before she did! There are two pages of information that you need to look at. You will need to figure out the clues on the next page before you can solve the piece of paper to the right. Anyway, you know what to do. I'm off to find more information about CodeCrusher and HideNSeek.

Good Luck,
Mr. SuperSneaky

— —

— — — — — — —

and

— — — — — .

— — — — — — —

— — — — — .

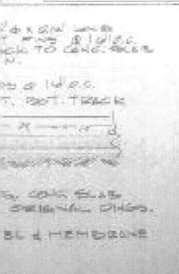
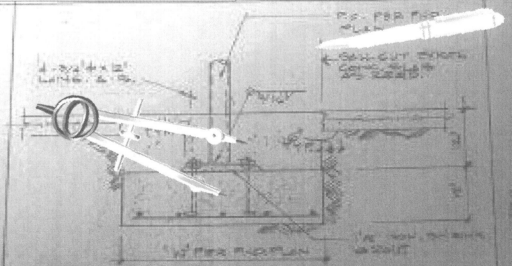

CHAPTER 29:

STAYIN' ON COURSE?

CRAZINESS

DUDE!

Go Read Proverbs 29

Ok, we know that we are supposed to listen to discipline and *instruction* from others. But what happens when you reach that period in your life when you don't feel like you are hearing any *instructions* from God? Often, in the Christian life, there will be times when God doesn't say yes to our prayers, or doesn't seem to be speaking to us in our quiet times. It can be very difficult, because you will start to doubt what is true. Even your relationship with God may seem fake and plastic. Those times are

BAD IDEA

If you see your life taking a turn for the worse STOP! Look for direction from God. Don't keep going down that path. You might get hurt!

bound to happen, but the question is: what will you do when you reach that time when nothing seems real? Are you just going to let your faith fizzle out? What are you supposed to do? Well, let's take a look at this, because if you don't think about this before it happens, your faith will be in great danger! OK, are you ready for this? You need to stay the course! Imagine that you are the captain of a **ship**. Now, let's say you're steering your **ship**. The best way to get where you're going

is to stay on course. The course of your **ship** is the path that you want your **ship** to journey on. How do you keep your **ship** from going somewhere that you don't want it to go? Stay on the course that you've set! If you stray from your course, you're going to end up in a place that you don't want to go. Don't go to the left or the right. Check out this verse:

Where there is no word from God, people are uncontrolled,
but those who obey what they have been taught are happy.
Proverbs 29:18 NCV

Continue to obey the stuff that you know is right and you will be blessed (happy). It can be tempting to run wild and do what everyone else is doing. But if you hold on to what you know, you won't go wrong. This is what Jesus told the church in Thyatira (thy-a-TIE-rah), which was struggling in its faith.

"Now I say to the rest of you in Thyatira, to you who do not hold to her teaching
and have not learned Satan's so-called deep secrets,
'I will not impose any other burden on you, except to hold on to what you have
until I come.'" Revelation 2:24-25 NIV

Stay firm, believer. Jesus is coming back very soon! That's Who you need to hold onto. Stay the course.

Verse of Fame

Proverbs 29:25

Fear of man will prove to be a snare, but whoever trusts in the LORD is kept safe.

Quiz 81

1. Think about a **ship**. If you were the captain and you learned that you were getting off track, you would try to get back on as fast as you could, right? What should happen when you learn that your life is getting off track?

2. What are some ways you can set your life back on track?

3. What is our God-given motivation to keep on the course?

4. What is one thing you learned from this section?

5. How are you going to apply what you learned today to your life?

Riddle Me This...

<u>Puzzle #1</u> – **DOT** DELIRIUM

Instructions for this game are found in Chapter 8, on page 71.

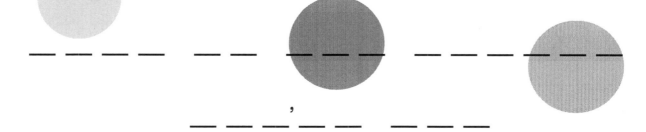

— — — —   — — — — —   — — — — —

,

— — — — —   — — —

Go Read Proverbs 29:1-15

If we forget what happens to wicked men, it will be very easy to fall prey to wickedness. Don't let that happen. You need to stay **firm**.

> *Whoever remains stiff-necked after many rebukes*
> *will suddenly be destroyed—without remedy.*
> *When the righteous thrive, the people rejoice;*
> *when the wicked rule, the people groan.*
> *Proverbs 29:1-2 NIV*

Do you ever feel like you get rebuked all of the time? And it seems like it is always for the same stuff? You need to yield in your heart. Listen to the rebuke and change. Don't let yourself remain "stiff-necked" (stubborn). Like that verse in the last chapter, always keep your hearts trembling before God. Be open to correction.

Let's take a look at the second verse. What does *that* mean? Well, think about who the most POPULAR kids in school are. The popular people can sometimes be really mean. When the POPULAR group ends up being a whole bunch of mean kids and bullies, people groan, especially the people who aren't "POPULAR." Unfortunately this is the situation in many schools, and maybe even in some churches. Now, I want you to think of the friendliest and nicest person that you know. Imagine if he was the leader of the POPULAR group. That would be pretty cool, wouldn't it? That's what that verse is saying. When bad people rule, people GROAN; but when good people rule, people rejoice.

Quiz 82

1. When you get rebuked for the same thing over and over, what should your response be?

2. How should our hearts always respond to correction?

3. Name two people that you would like to model your life after.

4. What is one thing you learned from this section?

5. How are you going to apply what you learned today to your life?

Riddle Me This...

Puzzle #2

Across ⟶

4. Keep your hearts _____ before God
5. You need to _____ in your heart.

Down ↓

1. Be open to _____
2. When we don't hear from God, we need to stay on _____
3. Whoever remains stiff-necked after many _____ will suddenly be destroyed

Course
Rebukes
Yield
Trembling
Correction

273

Go Read Proverbs 29:16-27

Alright gang, check out this verse.

> *Fear of man will prove to be a snare,*
> *but whoever trusts in the LORD is kept safe. Proverbs 29:25 NIV*

Are you ever terrified of people? Like maybe you're **AFRAID** of bad guys, gangsters, murderers, crooks, clowns, ballerinas, and politicians. Well God says not to be **AFRAID** of ANY man. The fear of man is like a trap. If you live your life in constant fear, it's like your fear is a trap that will capture you. God doesn't want this for His people. He wants you to live in freedom. He wants us to be free from fear. He's in control. If you trust in the Lord, He will keep you safe.

> *Where God's love is, there is no fear, because God's*
> *perfect love drives out fear.*
> *It is punishment that makes a person fear,*
> *so love is not made perfect in the person who fears.*
> *1 John 4:18 NCV*

Don't worry about anything. God has a plan for you, and He wants you to live in a way that you're trusting His plan. If you don't do this, it's like you're telling God that He's not big enough to protect you. He is big enough, and He wants you to rest in His perfect love. When we do, we will find peace. How do we stop being **AFRAID**? I used to be very fearful of a lot of things. How did I beat my fear? Well, I took some verses and memorized them. Then whenever I felt **AFRAID** I would read through them. Two of my favorite verses during this time were Isaiah 41:10, and Joshua 1:9. Memorize them, and then quote them to yourself whenever you are **AFRAID**. This really helped me conquer my fears.

Quiz 83

1. Does God want you to live in **FEAR** or *Freedom*?

2. What are some ways you can get out of the clutches of fear?

3. When you fear, what are you telling God? (Look at the end of this section.)

4. What is one thing you learned from this section?

5. How are you going to apply what you learned today to your life?

Real Life

Next time you are scared, remember that God doesn't want us to be scared of man. People can't hurt the only thing that really matters: your trust in Jesus. Jesus will ALWAYS take good care of you. Why would He do that? Because HE REALLY LOVES YOU!

Puzzle #3 – Code Crusher

Decoding directions contained in the letter... (just read the letter below)

SuperSpiesRUs.INC
321 SuperSneak Ln.
Hidden, Hiding 54321
1-800-ISPYONU

CONFIDENTIAL

Top Secret
This Letter Permitted to
Authorized Personnel Only

Dear CodeCrusher:

I haven't had much more luck in tracking down CodeMaker. I am still trying to figure out where the Head Quarters of WidGeTS is. Anyway, they are up to something. CodeMaker left this note for his son to bring to their headquarters. Obviously, an agent from our side picked it up before he did. Can you figure it out? I think it is scrambled....and the pictures and blanks are supposed to be words...one of them should rhyme with "snare". Once you fix the poem, circle the correct reference.

Good Luck,

Mr. SuperSneaky

3. This verse also says that the L ___ ___ D will keep us out of harm's way

1. This verse says that the ___ E ___ R of will be a snare

4. If we trust in him through all our days

2. To everyone who is scared of men like they are of a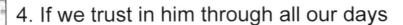

(a.) Proverbs 29:4   (b.) Proverbs 29:8
(c.) Proverbs 29:20 (d.) Proverbs 29:25

CHAPTER 30:

I Don't Want Money, But... I Do

Go Read Proverbs 30

Do you remember how I said that Proverbs had a few different authors? The first one was obviously Solomon. He wrote most of Proverbs 1-29. The last two chapters were written by two different men. The first one is Agur (AY-gur). He

 **Who Knew?**

Agur was in Ishmael's family. There are a lot of families in the Bible. You remember how we talked about David a little? Well, Jesus was in David and Solomon's family! How cool is that?

was believed to be a wise man or a scholar. Chapter 31 was written by King Lemuel (LEM-u-el). Both of these men were non-Jewish, which is kind of interesting, because the majority of the Old Testament is Jewish history and written by Jewish people. Agur is believed to be an Ishmaelite (Ishmael was Abraham's first son). Agur begins by saying that he has not gained wisdom. He's kind of doing a little bit of a pity party. He basically says, "I am so stupid! I'm not even smarter than the average human." Pity parties *can* be good, because it can mean that you have a broken heart before God; however, it's not good if you always feel bad or sorry for yourself or if you're pouting so that you can get attention. Remember that God wants us to live in the freedom

277

that comes from Him. We won't do a very good job of that if we are always feeling sorry for ourselves. Anyway, let's take a look at verse four:

> *Who but God goes up to heaven and comes back down?*
> *Who holds the wind in his fists?*
> *Who wraps up the oceans in his cloak?*
> *Who has created the whole wide world?*
> *What is His name—and His Son's name?*
> *Tell Me if you know!*
> *Proverbs 30:4 NLT*

There's this really powerful scene in Job, a book about a wealthy man named Job who Satan tempted; the cool part of the book is the fact that through all his hardship, he was faithful to God. Anyway, here's what happened - Job complained to God about the things that God tested him with. All of a sudden, God answered Job and said something pretty close to the verse we just read. Job had to face God and give an answer for why he was questioning God's wisdom. Agur is kind of doing the same thing. God is infinitely greater than we can ever imagine. He is in control. In some ways, we're kind of like little bugs to God; we are nothing compared to Him. He is far greater than any of us. But He still loves us. We need to come before Him in humility and listen to His instruction. If we don't, things will go badly for us.

Quiz 84

1. Name the three authors of Proverbs.

2. Sometimes we can be proud and think that we are in control instead of God. What are some different thoughts that we can put in the place of this wicked one?

3. How does God respond to our pride?

4. What is one thing you learned from this section?

5. How are you going to apply what you learned today to your life?

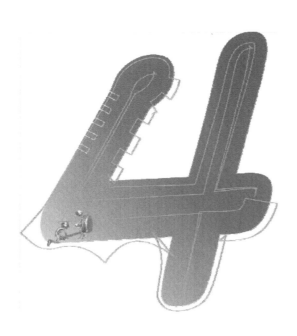

Verse of Fame

Proverbs 30:15b-16

"There are three things that are never satisfied, four that never say, 'Enough!': the grave, the barren womb, land, which is never satisfied with water, and fire, which never says, 'Enough!'

279

Riddle Me This…

<u>**Puzzle #1**</u> – NUMBER CODE

Find the words in the puzzle and write the remaining letters in the blanks.

```
H   C   E   H   R   H   A   V   E
A   U   O   G   U   U   B   R   O
K   E   M   N   A   M   G   N   A
N   D   H   I   T   R   A   A   U
M   B   L   E   L   R   E   N   H
E   A   R   T   B   I   O   V   E
L   E   U   M   E   L   T   L   A
F   O   R   E   G   O   D   Y   ☺
```

__ __ __ __   __

__ __ __ __ __ __

__ __ __

__ __ __ __ __ __

__ __ __ __ __

__ __ __ __ __ __

__ __ __

| Agur |
| Average |
| Control |
| Human |
| Humility |
| Lemuel |

280

Go Read Proverbs 30 Again

Agur prays the coolest prayer in this chapter. Do you feel utterly confused what to do with your money after Chapter 28? Maybe you have been wondering how you are able to let go of riches and not let your heart be captured by them. Check out Agur's prayer here:

> "I ask two things from you, LORD. Don't refuse me before I die. Keep me from lying and being dishonest. And don't make me either rich or poor; just give me enough food for each day. If I have too much, I might reject you and say, 'I don't know the LORD.' If I am poor, I might steal and disgrace the name of my God." Proverbs 30:7-9 NCV

So in his prayer, Agur asks God to give him two things. The very first thing out of his mouth is, "Don't let me lie!" He realizes that God hates it when we are DISHONEST and so he wants to be careful to be HONEST before God. The next thing he says is, "Don't let me be too rich or too poor." I think a lot of people would say, "God, let me have lots and lots of money so that I can get that new game! Oh yeah, *and* so I can give some food to those poor starving kids in Africa. Amen." That's not what Agur prays. He says, "And don't make me either rich or poor; just give me

Real Life

Pray and ask God to only give you what you need and that He would bless the others around you.

enough food for each day." Look at his reasons. He sees that when people get rich, their temptation is to think that they don't need God anymore. He wants to stay far away from that life. So then he turns to the poor and sees that they are often tempted to steal, so that they can have enough to eat. So he doesn't want that life either. So he prays, "God, put me right smack dab in the middle. I just want to please You!" How cool is that? The only thing that he wants to do is to glorify God. Do you have that kind of attitude? I often don't. It's tempting to want the newest cell phone, TV, video game, or clothes. But our attitudes need to be like Agur's attitude. Our only goal should be to please God. So if you don't know what to do with Chapter 28, you should pray this prayer. Now I realize that you probably only have around $3. But remember this stuff. Moses guessed that the Israelites would fall away from the Lord when there was plenty to eat (when they were RICH). Guess what? He was exactly right! So we need to make sure that the same thing doesn't happen to us. If you ever forget this, come back and read it again! It's important to make sure that we aren't destroyed by the same stuff that destroyed the Israelites!

Quiz 85

1. What two things does Agur pray for in his prayer?

2. Who guessed that the Israelites would fall?

3. What took the Israelites off track and made them stop trusting God?

4. What is one thing you learned from this section?

5. How are you going to apply what you learned today to your life?

Puzzle #2 – *Code Crusher*

Decoding directions contained in the letter... (just read the letter below)

SuperSpiesRUs.INC
321 SuperSneak Ln.
Hidden, Hiding 54321
1-800-ISPYONU

Top Secret
This Letter Permitted to
Authorized Personnel Only

Dear CodeCrusher:

As I was walking on the cold, winter streets of Hidden, Hiding, I found this flyer in a dirty ally. I sent it to you with the hope that you could make sense of it (it is on the next page). I think it was some information for the WidGeTS. I think I'll have to take a little trip to Codeworks, Concealed. I can't believe that it rained last night! If it hadn't, the identity of CodeMaker would be in our grasp! Although I do see that Thomas Michaels is the new vice president and HideNSeek is the new secretary of codes. I wonder what her last name is. I don't know about you, but I think that the WidGeTS corporation may be up to something way bigger than little pieces of paper with codes on them. Hmm, I wonder why it's important that they just got a lot of money. Are they going to buy something? And I think there might be a code in the middle of the flyer. Maybe it was to keep the WidGeTS spies busy. Nonetheless, if they have information, we need it. So crack that code!

Good Luck,
Mr. SuperSneaky

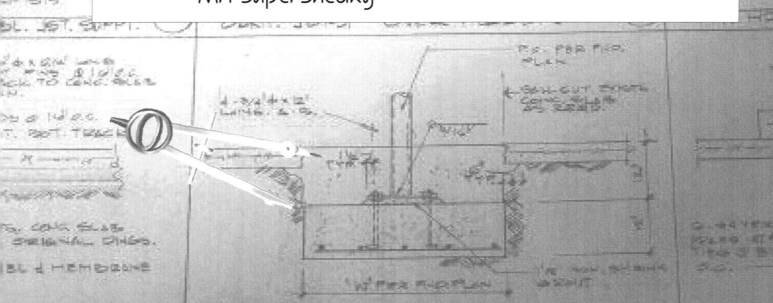

Attention all WidGeTS spies:
Relocating! We are going to be setting up our new headquarters in the small city of Codeworks, which is in the state of **Concealed**. We were donated a large amount of money by the NLRRA (National League of Racing Roadrunners Association). We are going to make the move in just a few days. Pack your bags to make your home in the beautiful city of Codeworks!

**PEKE EM MROF YILGN
NAD NIGEB HOSTNESID,
DNA TNOD KEMA EM
HERTIE HCRI RO OORP.**

— — — — — — — — — — — — — — — — —

— — — — — — — — — — — — — — — — —,

— — — — — — — — — — — — — —

— — — — — — — — — — — — — — — .

More important news:
We are going to have Mr. _____ (CodeMaker) become our president and Mr. _____ **Michaels** be our vice president. The board has decided that both men will be excellent leaders to acomplish our overall purpose. Also, Miss Miranda _____ (**HidNSeek**) will be our Secretary of Codes. Congradulations to all **three!**

WeGottheSecretINC

CHAPTER 31:

Serving like a CRAZY Whacko!

Go Read Proverbs 31:1-9

Wow! You have (almost) read through the whole book of Proverbs! That is incredible. Let me encourage you, if you skipped any of the readings, go back and read them. Proverbs is an incredible book, and you don't want to miss any of the *really* good stuff. Proverbs 31 is probably the most famous chapter of Proverbs. This chapter was written by *King* Lemuel. He basically writes the things that his mother taught him about being a

Who Knew?

The most famous chapter of Proverbs is Chapter 31. The funny thing is that Solomon didn't write it! Isn't that weird?

mother taught him about being a *king*. Did you know that you can train yourself to be great? Your name might not end up in future history books, but you can be a great man or woman of God. Can you think of a better way to train to be great than to train to be a *king*? Let's look at what *King* Lemuel's mommy has to say. She first tells him to be responsible with his life. Then she tells him to stay away from alcohol and beer, because she knows that they will destroy his life. Then she says something pretty cool:

God doesn't want only *kings* to stand up for the helpless – he wants you to as well. God wants *everyone* to stand up for the helpless. He wants you to be like a warrior in His army, and one of the biggest responsibilities of a warrior is to help the helpless. You need to do that. Be there for your siblings, friends, and *anyone* who can't stand up for themselves. If you do this, God will be pleased. Ok, I don't know if you're going to believe this, but that's not the famous part of Proverbs 31. Let's look at the very most famous part of Proverbs after these questions and a game!

Quiz 86

1. Who is Proverbs 31 written by?

2. Whose words is... um, *he*, writing down?

3. What did his mother tell him about standing up for people? Who specifically did she mention?

4. What is one thing you learned from this section?

5. How are you going to apply what you learned today to your life?

Riddle Me This...

<u>Puzzle #1</u> – **Block Brain!**

If you need a hint, take a look at Proverbs 31:8-9. This is the first block.

B E I	U S T I	E A K	A N N O	S E W	C E F
S P E A	O R T	N G C	E D .	T S P	E N S U
H O C	T H E M	F O R	R U S H	H O S E	T H O
S E L V	E S ;	R E J	F O R	K U P	

287

Go Read Proverbs 31:10-31

Ok, gang, I know that you aren't thinking about marriage, but you will think about it one day, and it will be incredibly important for you to be thinking about it in the right way. So we are going to be looking at the godly wife. Now kids, when you're older, you need to think about this correctly. Don't do what you want instead of following God's will. Here's what I mean by that: Let's say that in a few years when you're in school, you see a cute girl/guy. Ok, this is going to sound weird, but you need to be very careful about how you treat that person. Don't

Real Life

Wait for that special girl or guy! Let God's plan for your life guide your future. Don't try to rush it! You can keep yourself busy by serving in the church.

rush into a serious relationship. You're way to young for that anyway. Why? Because God is the perfect matchmaker. He already has a plan for who is going to be your husband/wife, and if you go around trying to force it, you're messing with God's perfect plan. When you hit high school, it will seem like everybody has a boy/girl friend. They run the risk of falling madly in love with the wrong person. Make up your mind right now, while you're still young, to let God lead you in His own timing. If you follow Him, you will find a lot more joy in your life.

Now, I know you're thinking, "This is weird." Good. Keep it that way! Anyway, the second part of Proverbs 31 is describing the godly wife. Gals, try to make this your goal in life. Be this woman. Guys, (when you're a lot older) look for this in your future wife, and you won't go wrong. So let's take a look at the godly wife.

> *It is hard to find a good wife, because she is worth more that rubies. Proverbs 31:10 NCV*

Girls, you could be like rare JEWELS! Remember when we talked about how godly lips are super rare? Well, the same is true of a godly wife. As you read through Proverbs 31, you see stuff like, "She gets up while it is still dark," "likes to work with her hands," "with money she earned, she plants a vineyard," and "She does her work with energy." Wow, that kind of makes her sound like a... servant! But think about this. God calls every Christian to have a servant's attitude. For almost eight years, I've gone to church about an hour before it starts. It's amazing to see all the people that get up early in the morning to make church happen. I mean, you've got the band members, sound guy/gal, PowerPoint dude, coffee person, cleaner guy, Sunday school teachers, pastor, window cleaner person... and some people do several of those jobs! Hardly anyone ever sees all the work that they put in. They're all servants. Whenever you get a chance, go to church really early some day and look at all of the servants there. You'll be surprised.

God wants you to serve like that with everyone: your family, friends, and classmates. You need to see yourself as their slave. Did you know that Jesus made the whole world? Did you know that Jesus is the King over all the earth? Did you know that Jesus made people? Did you know that Jesus washed His followers' feet? Can you imagine the U.S. President washing your feet? Yet GOD washed the feet of His followers! That's crazy! God wants us to imitate Him and be the servant of all.

Are you a servant? If you become good at serving, you will be one of the greatest people in the whole world. When we serve, God says, "Hey come over here, Michael. Look down there. No, no, right there... do you see little Johnny and Jenny down there? Yep, those kids are awesome! They serve me every single day." So if some of the things in Proverbs 31 seem confusing, all you need to do is just be a servant. If you do, you will have gotten something really great from Proverbs 31!

Quiz 87

1. Why are we telling you this stuff even though it isn't really important to you right now?

2. What are some ways that you can prepare yourself to be a good husband/wife?

3. When you see someone serving, you think *"That's cool. I wish I was like that."* How should this motivate us to serve? What are some ways that you can serve more today?

4. What is one thing you learned from this section?

5. How are you going to apply what you learned today to your life?

Verse of Fame

Proverbs 31: 30

Charm is deceptive, and beauty is fleeting; but a woman who fears the LORD is to be praised.

Puzzle #2 – Code Crusher

Decoding directions contained in the letter... (just read the letter below)

SuperSpiesRUs.INC
321 SuperSneak Ln.
Hidden, Hiding 54321
1-800-ISPYONU

Dear CodeCrusher:

You are not going to believe this: WidGeTS just moved to a gigantic building! I put a picture below of the building. It's unbelievable! They have guards all around the place, multiple floors, and they have a helicopter at their disposal! They also got 100 nice, new sports cars ready for each spy! It's unbelievable! I tried to get in, but instead of asking me questions, the guard just handed me an envelope with the papers on the next page in it. CodeCrusher, if you can solve this, we will have full access to their new building. It's up to you.

Good Luck,

Mr. SuperSneaky

P.S. – One more thing: we are also relocating to an office in the downtown part of Codeworks, Concealed. It has tons of features – it looks just like a normal house, but in reality, it has tunnels, high-tech computers two or three cars that look like old clunkers on the outside, but on the inside, they are high-tech spy vans! Now, we understand that you can't move with us, but we will continue to keep in touch. You're still part of the team!!!

From symbol to number

✡ ✝ ☪

___ ___ ___

👇 ✝ ✋ 👉 ☪ 💣 👆

___ ___ ___ ___ ___ ___ ___

👆 ☹

___ ___

☪ 🏴 🏴

___ ___ ___

From number to letter

___ ___   ___

___ ___ ___ ___ ___ ___ ___

___ ___

___ ___ ___

From backwards to forwards

___ ___   ___

___ ___ ___ ___ ___ ___

___ ___

___ ___ ___

A ~ V	A ~ 1	1 ~ 👈
B ~ U	B ~ 2	2 ~ 👉
C ~ T	C ~ 3	3 ~ ☝
D ~ S	D ~ 4	4 ~ 👇
E ~ R	E ~ 5	5 ~ ✋
F ~ Q	F ~ 6	6 ~ ☺
G ~ P	G ~ 7	7 ~ 😐
H ~ O	H ~ 8	8 ~ ☹
I ~ N	I ~ 9	9 ~ 💣
J ~ M	J ~ 10	10 ~ ☠
K ~ L	K ~ 11	11 ~ 🏴
L ~ K	L ~ 12	12 ~ 🏴
M ~ J	M ~ 13	13 ~ ✈
N ~ I	N ~ 14	14 ~ ☼
O ~ H	O ~ 15	15 ~ 💧
P ~ G	P ~ 16	16 ~ ❄
Q ~ F	Q ~ 17	17 ~ ✝
R ~ E	R ~ 18	18 ~ ✝
S ~ D	S ~ 19	19 ~ ✠
T ~ C	T ~ 20	20 ~ ✠
U ~ B	U ~ 21	21 ~ ✡
V ~ A	V ~ 22	22 ~ ☪

PROVERBS 32:

thE ENdiNG thiNGY

Go Read Proverbs 32

You're probably really confused and wondering what on earth is going on here. There is no Proverbs 32! Well, you're done. You've been through the entire book of Proverbs! Good job! It feels like we just started, doesn't it? Now, if you're like me, you're probably sitting there scratching your head and saying, "There are a lot of Proverbs! How am I supposed to remember all of the stuff that I've learned?" Well, one way to do that would be to memorize the entire book of Proverbs. Just kidding, but you might consider memorizing several of the key verses. And maybe when you're older, you *could* try memorizing the whole book. But for right now, maybe you could start out with your top ten favorite Proverbs and memorize those, or you could use the verses of fame and memorize a verse from every chapter! That would be pretty cool. But for now here is one practical thing that you could do: every morning try to set aside a devotional time - a time for just you and God. Now, how many chapters are in Proverbs? Thirty-one, right? Well, how many days are in a month? Thirty or thirty-one! What you could do is read a chapter of Proverbs a day. Then every month you would go through the whole book of Proverbs! For example, if I were to do that today, I would read Proverbs 25, because I'm writing this epilogue on August 25. Cool, huh? These are just a few ideas to keep Proverbs fresh in your mind. For the rest of this chapter, I want to review the most important things that we learned from reading Proverbs:

1. Remember that God sees what we do and that He always has a response for our actions. This is the fear of the Lord which is also the beginning of wisdom. The whole book of Proverbs looks at the consequences of our actions.

2. We learned about the importance of listening to Wisdom, and the blessings that come with it. We also took a look at what happens when we don't listen to Wisdom and follow our own ways.

3. We took a look at our reputation. We saw how it affects God, our parents, friends, and everybody around us. It is important that we do stuff that is honorable so that we will keep a good reputation.

4. We saw the importance of watching our speech. We need to make sure that our speech is a blessing to all of those around us.

5. We saw the importance of being hard workers in order to give God a good reputation. When we are lazy and don't work hard, we set ourselves up for failure.

6. Remember the importance of always telling the truth. Nothing about God is false, so He wants us to make sure that nothing about us is false. We are His ambassadors to the whole world. We need to be doing a good job!

7. We were warned in several chapters against the love of money. When we chase after riches, we see that they disappear. The joy that we think they will bring us is just a false promise. Instead of searching for riches, we should be seeking God and learning to grow in Him.

8. Remember that we need to be honest and loyal to our friends. In order to be a good friend, we need to do stuff that benefits our friends more than ourselves.

9. We saw the importance of serving in our future marriages, with our friends, at home, and everywhere in between. Jesus gave us the ultimate demonstration of serving when He died on the cross. We need to have that kind of attitude when serving our family and friends.

10. Finally, we learned about trusting God. When we trust God with our lives, we are surrendering ourselves to Him. When we surrender ourselves to God, we are letting Him be the King of our lives. This is God's rightful place. Incredible good comes from having God be the King of your life.

Of course, we learned much, much more, but these are the top ten points that we talked about. Remember to keep your heart, ears, and eyes open to God's work in your life.

We had a lot of fun putting this together for you, and we hope that your lives are different because of this book. We pray that you learned a lot of stuff while reading this, but more importantly, we pray that you're closer to God. Thanks for taking this journey through Proverbs with us.

The Nelson Kids

GOSPEL:

The Answer to the BIG Question

Alright, you're probably here because of Chapter 9 or you just finished the study. If you finished the study: Good job! In our study, we've talked a lot about choosing wisdom and God. What does this really mean? Well, let me try to show you. OK, so we all know that God is love (1 John 4:8), and that God is perfect (keep that in mind). But we also know that God is just (or fair); He treats everyone the same. OK, what about you? We know what God is like, but what are people like? Well, we are disobedient. Imagine a whole flock of sheep. Now this flock is busy chewing grass and being watched over by a shepherd. One sheep says to another, "Hey, we don't need this shepherd guy. Let's go do our own thing." All of a sudden, the whole flock decides to do the exact same thing, and they all run away from the shepherd at the exact same time. That's what we're like with God. We say, "Hey, I don't need your help, so see you later, alligator." Every single person has done this to God in their heart.

OK, what's so bad about that? When we choose not to follow God, we are really choosing sin over God. But that's not even the worst part of it. When we sin, God can't be around us! Why? Because God is completely holy.

> *Your eyes are too pure to look on evil;*
> *You cannot tolerate wrongdoing. Habakkuk 1:13a NIV*

OK, let's say that you're like a pizza to God. Now let's say that *every* time you sin, you add a little dog poo-poo to your pizza. Now, how many times do you have to add dog poo-poo before the pizza is bad? Only once, right? Nobody wants to eat

296

pepperoni and poo-poo pizza! Eww. Well, that's what it's like with God. All we have to do is sin once and we need to be thrown away. Our biggest problem of all is that the trash can is hell.

Now there's got to be some way out of this, right? Well, what some people try to do is say, "All you have to do to get into heaven is to do good things. Then God will let you into heaven."

 OK, let's see if that's the right way to view it. Back to the pizza. Let's say that every good thing that you do is like adding a little bit of good toppings onto the pizza. Let's imagine that you say a kind word to your sister (add a little cheese), you help your mom (add some pepperonis), and you read your Bible (add some sausage). There, that should do it. The pizza is good now. Wait a second! Don't eat it: remember that you still have poo-poo on your pizza! Does adding more cheese really make you want to eat it? Not really. It's still disgusting. Now some people say, "No, no, no. If you add enough good stuff on your pizza, you won't notice the bad stuff." Yeah, right! I don't care how much cheese you put on that pizza, I'm not eating it! And God won't take it either.

So we're in a pretty bad place. There's no way that we can get rid of our "poo-poo" (our sins). People are always asking this question, "How can a loving God send good people to hell?" Well, think about it. We all have poo-poo on our pizza. Some people have more than other people, but everyone still has at least a little bit on their pizza. Because God is perfect, He can't be around us: He's got to throw away the pizza. But the people who ask that question do have a point: how can God be loving and still send us to hell? Well, He provided a way for us to get rid of our sins. Jesus came down from heaven and took away all our sins on the cross. He got rid of them. He made it so that we don't have to have poo-poo on our pizza. When you get to know Jesus (We'll talk about that after these next questions), Jesus makes you into someone completely new. Instead of pepperoni and poo-poo pizza, He makes you into the best dessert pizza you've ever tasted before in your life.

297

Let me try to explain this more clearly. Let's say that you go to a new school. You decide that you want to try and be as bad as you can. So you push little kids down the slide, punch people in the face, and you even break a little boy's arm. Well, a teacher comes out and takes you to the principal's office. You walk in and see that it's your dad's best friend who used to come to your house all the time. He looks at you, smiles, and says, "Look, you really messed up out there. I would like to let you go, but I have to be fair. You either need to be expelled from school, or you need to pay the families for all the damage that you have done, which comes out to $2,500."

Now, you definitely don't have that kind of money, so that means that you're through at that school. You turn to leave, but the principal puts his hand on your shoulder and says, "Look, I love you, but I have to be fair to everyone. So here's what I'll do. I'll give you the $2,500." He pulls out his wallet and holds out the money.

WOW! Isn't that cool? Now all that's left to do is take the $2,500. That's what Jesus did. When all hope seemed lost, He came down from heaven and paid the price. All that's left for us to do is to take the gift. How do you do that? How do you say "yes" to God's offer to pay for your sins? Check out what this verse says:

> "That if you confess with your mouth, Jesus as Lord, and believe in your heart that God raised Him from the dead, you will be saved."
> Romans 10:9 NASB

So, here's all that you have to do: you just have to pray. You can either pray your own prayer, or if you want some help, just pray something like the one in the scroll below:

> "Dear Jesus, I know that I've really messed up. I can never get rid of the sin that's in my life. But I know that You can. I want You to take over my life and get rid of my sin. I want to follow Wisdom and especially You. Thanks for Your gift. In Jesus' name, Amen."

Now if you prayed this and meant it, and if you believe that Jesus is the Son of God and that He died on the cross to pay for your sin, you no longer have any poo-poo on your pizza. Jesus has freed you from all your sin. And you'll never have any poo-poo on your pizza ever again. Even if you sin more, God will forgive you! You're free from sin! How cool is that? OK, if this all makes sense, go find your mom and dad, and tell them about what you just did. They can help you take the next steps. Very cool. If you *haven't* finished the study, GET GOING!! And if you have finished it all, maybe you could read it all over again...

Quiz 87

1. What is some poo-poo that you've put on your pizza?

2. How do you think you get the gross stuff off your pizza?

3. Can you ever add enough good toppings (good things) on your pizza to cover the dog poo-poo (our sins)? Would you ever eat a pizza with dog poo-poo? Would God like a life that is full of sins?

4. Why does a loving God send good people to hell? (Hint: I answered this exact question already on page 297!)

Made in the USA
Charleston, SC
19 December 2011